# Language and the Teacher: A Series in Applied Linguistics

*Volume 16*

under the editorial direction of

DR. ROBERT C. LUGTON

American Language Institute of New York University

LANGUAGE AND THE TEACHER:
A SERIES IN APPLIED LINGUISTICS

The series will be concerned with the following areas—

GENERAL STUDIES
Psycholinguistics, sociolinguistics, bilingualism.

GRAMMAR
Morphology, syntax, contrastive structure.

PHONOLOGY
Phonemics, intonation, contrastive phonetics, etc.

VOCABULARY STUDIES
Frequency counts, production and principles, lexicology.

READING SKILLS
Beginning skills, development, construction of texts, literary reading.

WRITING SKILLS
Beginning skills, development, composition.

METHODOLOGY
Evaluation of methods, techniques, classroom practices.

LANGUAGE TEACHING
FOR DIFFERENT AGE GROUPS
Elementary, secondary, college, adult.

MACHINE TEACHING
Programmed learning, audio-visual equipment and software, language laboratory.

TEACHER EDUCATION
Standards and evaluation, projects, curricula for teacher training

ADMINISTRATION
Curriculum development, articulation, public relations.

TESTING
Techniques, statistical studies.

BIOGRAPHY

BIBLIOGRAPHY

ENGLISH AS A SECOND LANGUAGE

METHODS OF RESEARCH IN LINGUISTICS
AND LANGUAGE TEACHING

*Language and the Teacher:*
*A Series in Applied Linguistics*

# Toward a Practical Theory of Second-Language Instruction

by

Philip D. Smith, Jr., Ph.D.
West Chester State College

THE CENTER FOR CURRICULUM DEVELOPMENT, INC.
401 Walnut Street Philadelphia, Pa.
#2788

For Ray McGuire, Tom Wells, Edward Allen, and Emanuel Berger—all of whom helped me at a critical juncture.

"... it is necessary to study the question of how an organism ... determines from various kinds of linguistic data, heard sentences, contexts, corrections, the particular manifestation of this theory used in the community..."

Paul Postal
"Underlying and Superficial Linguistic Structures"



First edition



Published in Philadelphia by The Center for Curriculum Development, Inc.

and simultaneously in Canada by
Marcel Didier Canada, Ltée
ISBN 0-8384-2788-X

Manufactured in the United States of America by Success, Inc.

# Contents

| | |
|---|---|
| INTRODUCTION | 1 |
| The Pendulum Swings . . . | 3 |
| A Taxonomy of Second-Language Education | 5 |
| THE CHANGING SCENE | 9 |
| A MODEL OF LEARNING | 13 |
| Carroll's Model of Language Learning | 16 |
| Creative Behavior | 17 |
| Motivation | 18 |
| LINGUISTICS | 21 |
| Implications from Linguistics and Psycholinguistics | 26 |
| Relationship Between First and Second Languages | 28 |
| STAGES IN LANGUAGE LEARNING | 31 |
| BASIC PROPOSITIONS FOR AN INSTRUCTIONAL APPROACH | 36 |
| BASIC PROPOSITIONS FOR FORMULATION OF A CLASSROOM APPROACH | 38 |
| PRACTICAL APPLICATIONS OF PSYCHOLINGUISTIC INSIGHTS | 40 |

Language Instruction: A Generative Approach 46
Hierarchy of Interrogation 51
Theoretical Bases for Course Progressions 58
Course Progression Bases—Model Peace Corps Courses 61
Criteria for Instructional Materials 62
Criteria for a Pedagogical Unit 66
Practical Pedagogical Unit 68
Sample Pedagogical Units 70
Dialogue Africain Contemporain 83
Cultural Notes 92
A Generative Approach—One More Time 101
Does it Work? 102
References 104

# Introduction

It is not often that a foreign-language educator is given *carte blanche* to create new and innovative foreign-language programs with adequate financing and a guaranteed opportunity to test and revise materials. I was fortunate to have had this opportunity from 1969 to 1971 on behalf of the Peace Corps.

Most of the thinking and much of the writing of this book is a direct result of involvement in directing the development of model instructional programs for the Peace Corps in French for Africa, Brazilian Portuguese, and Korean. This has been both a challenging and rewarding assignment.

The charge to build exemplary courses from "the ground up" encouraged extensive reading and a prolonged examination of the foreign language "state of the art" as it entered the 1970's. I am deeply indebted to the many friends with whom I have agreed, and often differed, but from whose insights I have always benefitted. I am particularly thankful to my associates John Harvey, Lee Sparkman, Maria Chapira, and Charles Heinle, and to John

Francis, former director of Language Training, Peace Corps.

Here, I make no pretense of originality, my aim has solely been to state—at a nuts-and-bolts level—a more productive and practical approach to second-language teaching that has proven to be highly effective.

Philip D. Smith, Director
Peace Corps Materials Project
CCD, Philadelphia

## THE PENDULUM SWINGS . . .

No area of the curriculum seems as beset by new approaches and subsequent reactions as foreign languages. For over a decade, the trend in both techniques, materials, testing, and audio-visual equipment has been the now well-known audio-lingual approach. As the profession closes the "Audio-lingual Decade" and enters another, enough serious questions have been raised about the audio-lingual approach to warrant a new examination of the theoretical bases for second-language learning in a formal educative process.

The audio-lingual approach to foreign-language learning had, by the mid-1960's, gained widespread acceptance by both the profession and supporting laymen as the most effective strategy for the development of second-language skills. With dissemination and impetus provided by the National Defense Education Act, foreign-language teaching underwent both dramatic and traumatic changes. Yet, at precisely the same point in time when "audio-lingualism" was making its greatest strides toward widespread acceptance, concerned specialists in the psychology of language learning were pointing out that many of the basic assumptions on which the audio-lingual approach is predicated do not agree with the realities of efficient learning in the school environment.

While the basic assumption that foreign-language learning is primarily a mechanical process of habit formation was early challenged by Chomsky (1959) in his review of B. F. Skinner's *Verbal Behavior,* this theoretical discussion was remote from the classroom until the publication of Wilga Rivers' stimulating *The Psychologist and the Foreign Language Teacher* in 1964. Rivers pointed out four major assumptions of the audio-lingual approach that did not agree with current thinking in psychology: (1) foreign-language learning is a process of habit formation; (2) speech should precede writing; (3) learning should be through analogy rather than analysis; and (4) meaning should be taught in a cultural context (i.e., without English).

David Ausubel challenged the assumptions of the audio-lingual approach for mature learners in the pages of the *Modern Language Journal* (Ausubel, 1964). John Carroll pointed out to foreign-language educators that "... the audio-lingual habit theory which is so prevalent in American foreign-language teaching was, perhaps, fifteen years ago, in step with the state of psychological thinking at that time, but it is no longer abreast of recent developments ... " (1965, p. 281). Beverly Bazan called the attention of the profession to "The Danger of Assumption Without Proof" (1964) in adoption of new classroom practices and pointed out with reference to audio-lingual teaching that:

> Very little controlled research has been done on the assumptions of this methodology with specific reference to the secondary language learning situation. General research, however, raises several questions with respect to these assumptions ... (1964, p. 337).

As late as 1966, Nelson Brooks, leading theoretician of the audio-lingual movement admitted:

> Up to the present, what is called the new approach is largely an act of faith; research to prove the validity of its basic principles is scanty. It is, however, an act of faith of vast dimensions ... If research data are in short supply, it is mainly because the scientific measurement of what is sought is extremely difficult and because the needed instruments have, up to now, not been available ... (1966, p. 359).

The same year, Albert Valdman lent weight to the generative view when he pointed out to foreign-language educators that "the most serious shortcoming of New Key materials is that they constitute a closed system" (Valdman, 1966, p. xix).

Guillermo del Olmo (1967), commenting on the audio-lingual approach in *Foreign Language Annals,* the journal of the American Council of the Teaching of Foreign

Languages, called for a reexamination of the accepted methodology, stating:

> We should examine the list of characteristics of the audio-lingual approach that have been isolated by Rivers (1964), Scherer and Wertheimer (1964), and Valdman (1966), and show how these characteristics fare in the pragmatic atmosphere of the classroom (p. 28).

The large-scale Pennsylvania Foreign Language Research Projects (Smith, 1970), the comparison of Chastain, and the Swedish GUME Projects (Olsson, 1969), were among those at the close of the decade which challenged the increased effectiveness once posited for the audio-lingual approach in the formal education setting. Recently, Jakobovits (1970) has convincingly challenged the logical assumptions of the audio-lingual teaching strategy.

It is not the thesis of this present work to either belittle or belabor a movement that did inestimable good in the revitalization of a sagging discipline. Rather, the purpose is to examine the contributions of pertinent fields over the second half of the past decade to better develop a new perspective. Upon this can be built classroom practices for more efficient second-language learning in the formal instructional setting. The first step in this process must be a discussion of the scope involved in the parameter "second-language learning in the formal instructional setting".

## A Taxonomy of Second-Language Education

Second-language learning in the formal instructional process occurs in four dimensions: school level, type of individual involvement, the depth of language mastery, and chronological time. The relative location of each of these can best be visualized as in Figure 1.

The four stages of language acquisition are Beginning, Intermediate, Advanced, and Continuing. Their boundaries are subjective and ill-defined, the divisions vague and largely dependent on the administrative viewpoint. The concept of the Continuing phase has not yet been widely discussed but holds promise as a theoretical justification for skills maintenance programs at the graduate and professional levels.

Educational levels in the American/European tradition are the elementary years, a secondary preparatory school, and the university. To this must be added the "specialized" language training programs of government, industry, the military, and others. One can begin mastery of a second language at any of these levels although it is difficult to conceive of most learners proceeding beyond the Beginning stage at the elementary level or the Intermediate stage at the secondary. Both the University and Specialized levels can lead into the Advanced stage and the Continuing phase which is usually encountered in a professional real-life situation. Each of these steps must be successive along both the skills and time continuums.

The fundamental "building blocks" of the second-language learning process are, of course, the individuals concerned. The whole structure rests upon the *learner*—without him there is no need for the others. Most directly influencing the learner is the *teacher.* His role places him as the mediator between the theoretician, the language, and the learner.

Overlooked, but important, is the program *administrator.* This supervisor sets policy that facilitates, inhibits or prevents the language-learning process. His role should not be minimized in the hierarchy of human involvement.

Above the basic local level lie the lighter theoretical courses of the *linguist,* the *psychologist,* and the *research specialist.* The linguist and the psychologist provide information on the nature of the language and on the learning process to the teacher-administrator team. While the contributions of both of these sciences may vary at any given moment, their existence is undeniable.

The educational research specialist is the evaluator at each stage and level of the process. He cannot perform his task until the others have each done theirs. His position is more remote, his influence least, on the actual learning tasks.

Figure.1. A Taxonomy of Second-Language Education

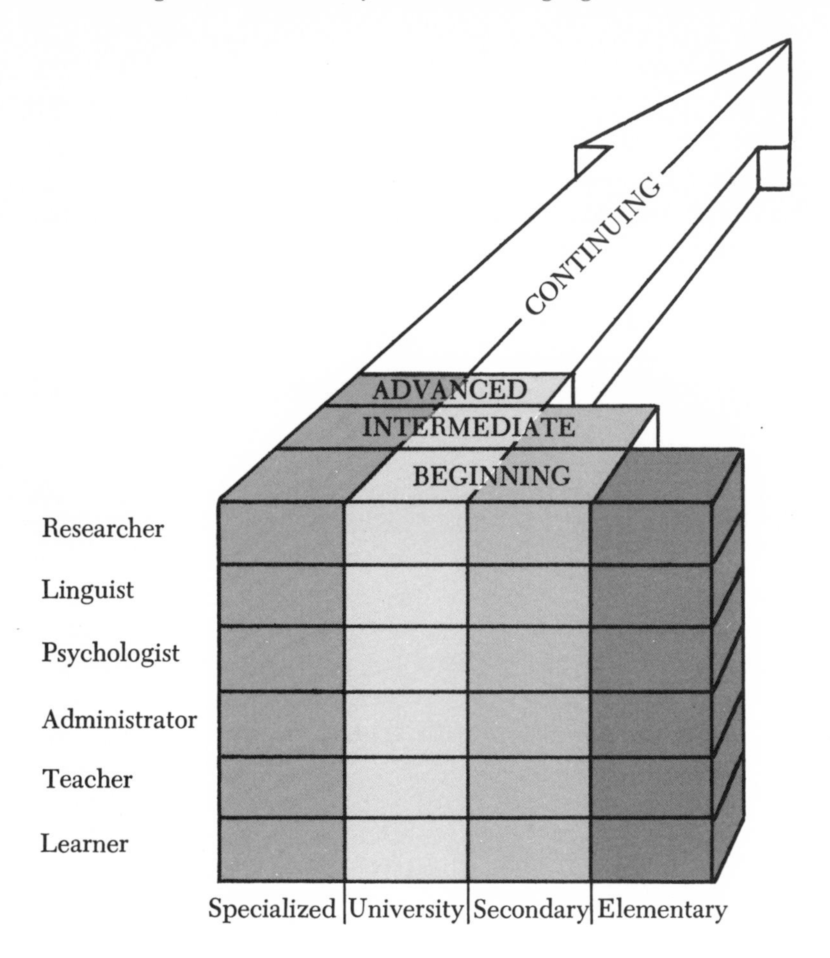


Although several roles can be assumed by one individual or each individual can act rather independently, the relationships hold true. The "self-taught" learner either assumes the role of "mediator"—teaches himself—or utilizes materials carefully constructed by a teacher in another time and space. The researcher must have subjects to measure—the administrator, programs to supervise.

The time continuum must remain unspecified. The elementary-school student might spend a few minutes each day for several years while the Peace Corps Trainee in an intensive in-country program may cover the same linguistic material in a matter of days or weeks. Second-language mastery is cumulative and linear, but concerned individuals will all devote different times to each step in the process.

# The Changing Scene

"Challenge and change" is the slogan of the majority of the language learners who are now the clientele of the profession. Biologically, sociologically, spatially, and psychologically, the learner is on the move. The foreign-language educator must not only be aware of both the change and its direction but also incorporate this knowledge to facilitate instruction.

It is amply evident that a new generation of language learners face the teacher. The FLES student has learned more from television than from books, the secondary student may be a budding militant "tuning out" all he considers "not relevant", the university student is of the Woodstock rather than the New Frontier, and a Peace Corps psychologist in Brazil laments the passing of the crusading zeal of the Volunteer of the "good old days" of 1962.

No discussion of second-language education can focus on the learner without examining both the *psychology of learning* and the *cultural milieu* in which the learner exists. Both of these disciplines, educational psychology and sociology, are by definition astable. Each discipline is a growing organism—as new techniques and insights appear—devoted to the study of evolving phenomena—the learner and his culture.

It seems wisest for the foreign-language educator to constantly reassess the instructional process in light of change. The implications for flexibility in techniques and materials are obvious. In a statement already cited, Carrol pointed out in 1964 that widely accepted approaches were based on psychological thinking already fifteen years out of date.

A knowledge gap is understandable between the theoretical/experimental psychologist and the classroom foreign-language teacher. An even larger time differential exists between the theoretician and the creation, publication, dissemination, and evaluation of instructional materials. This delay of more than a decade is inefficient and fast becoming intolerable as society evolves at an ever increasing rate.

As an illustration, the audio-lingual approach to language teaching had theoretical bases on psychological and linguistic insights of the late 1940's and 1950's. These saw fruition and popularization through the writings of Fries, Brooks, and Lado with dissemination via the Modern Language Association and the National Defense Education Act. Concurrently, psychologists and linguists of the stature of Bruner and Chomsky had already advanced new theoretical bases. Evaluation of the audio-lingual approach did not take place until the end of the 1960's and was received with considerable disbelief by the profession. Revised materials, such as the completely reoriented second edition of the *Audio-Lingual Materials,* appeared exactly ten years after their original popularization via the first NDEA Institutes.

The theoretical-implementation and implementation-evaluation gaps can be reduced in several ways. The first, obviously, is better communication between theoretician and practitioner. The second, an instructional strategy which includes *immediate* evaluation and revision for improvement rather than delayed assessment.

The exchange of ideas among theoreticians and practitioners has undergone considerable improvement during the 1960's. This can be attributed in part to the increasing willingness of the theoretician to work more within the framework of the reality of the human community and to write in a manner more easily read by the practitioner.

More credit must go to the increasing sophistication of the practitioner and the emergence of a new professional type, the foreign-language educator, literate in both the disciplines of learning and linguistics and dedicated to translation of the implications of both at the instructional level.

Recognition must also be made of the contributions of the professional journals and societies toward the improvement of increased communication between theoretician and practitioner. Older journals are now devoting more content to pedagogy. New publications have emerged to absorb some of the backlog of worthwhile information. Editors are accepting fewer testimonials and publishing provocative but readable articles on the psychological and linguistic issues of second-language learning. Abstracting, microfilming and a growing "research awareness" in the practitioner have made the reader more knowledgable and receptive.

Professional associations have expanded their interests to include sessions on pedagogy and linguistics in addition to their more traditional interests in literary studies. Membership involves the practitioner to a far greater degree than in past generations—witness the tremendous growth of the Northeast Conference and its imitators. The American Council on the Teaching of Foreign Languages provides a profession-wide inter-language forum. Meetings at the state and local levels are more and more dedicated to relevance to the instructional process. The number and quality of in-service programs for teachers is slowly improving.

The wide acceptance of the systems approach with its emphasis on immediate evaluation and system adjustment has reduced the delay between the creation and improvement of programs. This is most certain to continue. The result has been the more wide-spread acceptance of evaluation strategies such as Egon Guba's aexperimental approach (1965), constant curriculum revision during the instructional process; the development of criterion-referenced program-specific measurement; and short-term evaluation studies. The increasing availability of the computer for both high-speed test scoring and quick statistical analyses has facilitated the acceptance and enhanced the value of immediate revision.

# A Model of Learning

The mental processes involved in learning have been discussed in depth by educational psychologists. Any introductory text in this field will mention and attempt to delineate the role of perception of stimuli, the needs and motivations of the learner, his cognitive storage of knowledge, the affective evaluative component, and the response elicited as these merge into an active command from the mind to the body. The immediate correction of inappropriate responses reveals a self-evaluative "feed-back" line used to keep the learner within the parameters he desired.

The exact relationship of each of the major components—motivation, cognition, evaluation, and response formation—is a matter of shifting debate among psychologists and undeniable shifts from moment to moment within the human organism itself. An appropriate formal model of the learning process is relatively simple if one understands that the true complexity can never be either fully known nor graphically captured. These same components at work within the minds of both author and reader will preclude universal response.

A simple model of the learning process seems to resemble the mechanism of the jet engine. A large mass of air is guided toward the engine by the input cone. This narrows to an orifice which permits only selected amounts of air to enter. Once inside the engine, the air is mixed with a steady fuel, churned by an impellor and ignited. The resulting hot expanded gas is thrust out the rear, imparting in a forward motion to the engine. An external guidance system adjusts for the correct speed and direction.

Figure 2

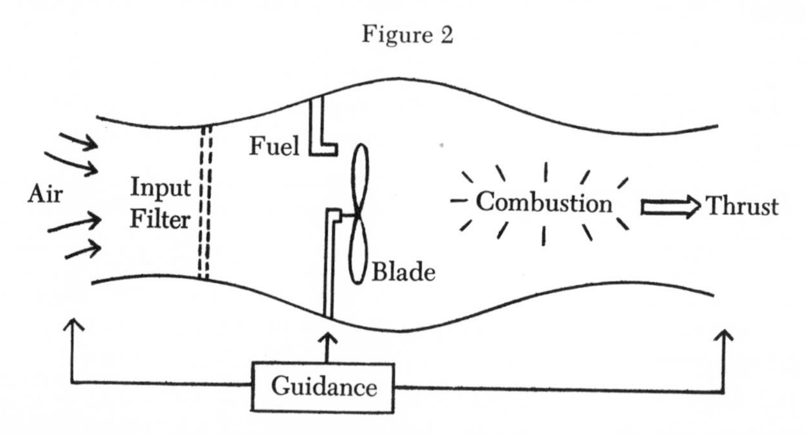


It seems appropriate to substitute the mental process of the learner in this same configuration:

Figure 3

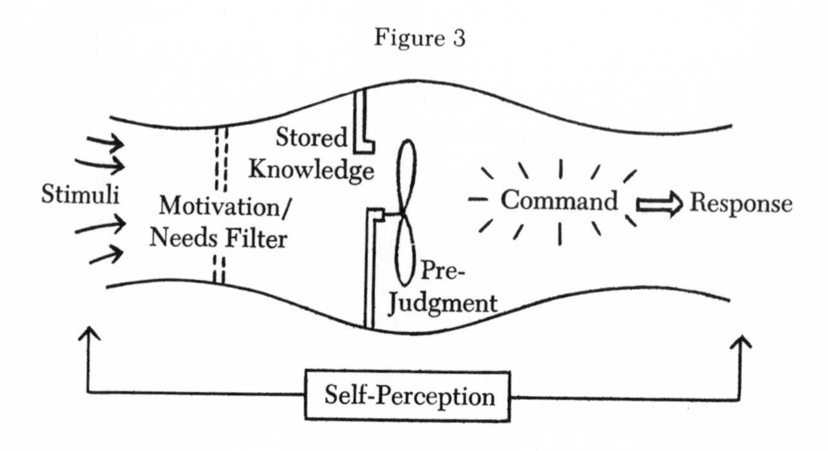

Here the stimuli are scanned by the learner and received by him as he perceives them to be important in terms of his felt needs and motivations, only admitting those which he perceives to be relevant. The received perceptions are then mixed with pertinent "known facts" stored from prior experiences, churned by the subjective interpretations that are an inherent part of each human. The mixture results in (usually) some type of physical response (absence of response is also response). The appropriateness of the response is evaluated by the learner as his behavior modifies the situation around him. A more formal statement of the model is shown in Figure 4.

Figure 4

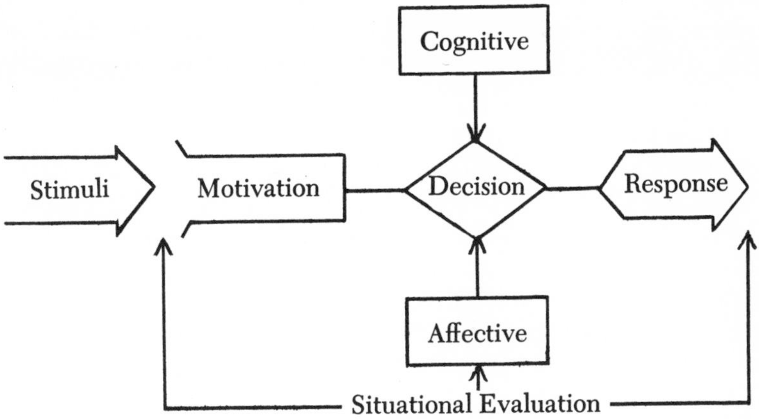

Cognitive
Stimuli
Motivation
Decision
Response
Affective
Situational Evaluation

Recently a new term has been coined to reinforce the concept that it is the internal process which deserves emphasis rather than the more external behavioristic concept of Stimulus-Response. Here "Input" and "Output" are placed in their proper perspective as "peripheral" by the term *throughput,* which emphasizes the internal processes of cognitive thinking.

It becomes quickly evident that the most important factor governing learning is the importance attached to it by the learner. Unless relevance is perceived, meaningful learning will not take place. This is supported by the model of language learning advanced by Carroll (1963) in which learning is defined in terms of student perseverance—how long he sticks with it—the external evidence of internal motivation.

## Carroll's Model of Language Learning

In his well-known chapter in Gage's *Handbook of Research on Teaching* (1963), John Carroll proposed a conceptual model of foreign-language learning which included: 1) aptitude, 2) general intelligence, 3) the learner's perseverance, 4) the quality of instruction, and 5) opportunity.

Aptitude and intelligence have often been posited as constants in the instructional process. That such is not necessarily true can be evidenced by a learning-mode preference felt by some individuals—one may be "apt" via one medium and "less apt" via another—and the verbal:non-verbal distinction made in intelligence testing. The implications for providing a learner with a variety of stimuli designed to teach the same linguistic patterns is evident.

Figure 5. A Model of Language Learning (after Carroll)

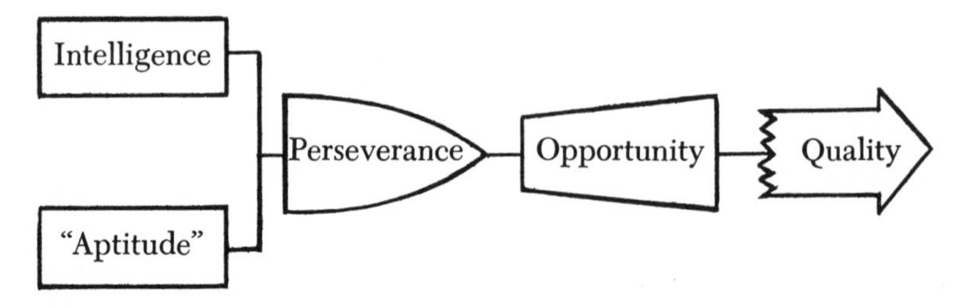


Perseverance is a reflection of motivation; the quality of instruction should, but often does not, capitalize on the expressed needs and interests of the learner. Opportunity is a curriculum function usually emasculated by traditional educational systems. A true concern with relevant foreign-language programs and freedom to provide optimum curricular planning for learning can achieve better success than programs generally do—witness Peace Corps successes which even in themselves need further improvement.

It might, at this point, be appropriate to point out that a theory of second-language instruction may well take the form of a non-structured entity, to encourage the maximization of each component within a selection range which the learner perceives to be meaningful to him, a grab-bag of curricular components made available to the learner by the mediator. The best theory may be that there should be as many theoretical curricula as there are learners.

This thought is merely an echoing of the already hallowed "individual needs and interests" cliché of educationists. It is, however, a viable concept and fully worthy of pursuit within the framework of, first, sincerity—does one really seek individualization—and, second, practicality—can it be realistically obtained. Most recent curricular attempts in several disciplines seem to have compromised, ten percent on sincerity, ninety percent on the reality of traditional curricular patterns. The reverse should be true.

To provide for the circumvention of the traditional curriculum patterns of the formal education process, a second-language learning program must be designed for success within total flexibility. No mean task . . .

## Creative Behavior

The application of well-known tenets of educational psychology to second-language learning can be easily seen. The mind is known to be constantly busy classifying, interpreting, and storing information for future recall and use. Verbal input is probably sorted at several levels commensurate with the syntactic, lexical, and semantic levels of the learner's inherent linguistic competence.

Items, once classified, are then interpreted by the formation of generalizations about their relationships with other already sorted concepts. Lastly, these are stored in the human mind in an associative relationship with other concepts so that recall of one brings others into consciousness.

Chomsky (1959) has long since refuted the behavioristic viewpoint of language acquisition at the theoretical level. That second-language use is a conscious problem-solving process of high order is easily observable in the painstaking attempts of a less-than-fluent but intelligent learner. Here the communications block is clearly a problem to be solved. The painstaking effort, the obvious mental lexical sorting, the correction of errors after utterance, and ingenious circumlocutions amply demonstrate cognitive thinking at work.

The behaviorist approach would concentrate on drilling common basic surface patterns of language until they become fully automatic. This can be done within a well-defined set of utterances but can never realize the automatic control of novel utterances. Even the best qualified native speaker sometimes finds himself searching for appropriate phrases or at a loss for words. The poet, of course, is the master of these skills.

Since cognitive use of language is undeniable, it seems prudent to teach the learner to capitalize on the process at an early stage. Certainly, it increases his interest and sharpens his perceptive abilities. If it is true that "Creative behavior is always original behavior" (McDonald, 1965, p. 302), then the reverse is also true, "Original behavior is creative behavior". The same author states that "Creativity is learned"—*ergo,* original behavior is learned/can be taught.

Since original verbal behavior is important in actual communications situations, it is incumbent upon the instructional process to provide the learner with early opportunities to practice this skill. Early encouragement to be creative in a sheltered instructional environment will lessen the trauma certain to come when faced with a novel situation in a different culture.

### Motivation

It is in the area of motivation that foreign-language educators have been least successful. It can be amply demonstrated that strong motivation can work wonders in compensating for lack of inherent ability. The handicapped can overcome his physical problem; the serious student can achieve better than a more intelligent but lazy counterpart;

the zealot can overcome shyness; tenacity can overcome hardship. A thousand examples could be cited.

Lack of success in capitalizing on motivation can be attributed to a number of factors, beginning with a lack of clarity about the role of motivation itself. Frymier (1968) has discussed the construct of motivation in some depth, annotating several hundred studies of motivation in the educational setting. Not one deals with second-language learning.

Pimsleur (1962), after a search of the literature, commented that the influence of motivation on second-language learning appeared to be "consistent from the scanty evidence . . . " (p. 167).

Motivation, as described by Frymier, lends itself to binary notation, *plus* and *minus, high* and *low.* Especially important is the concept of *avoidance motivation* as a reciprocal of the positive drive often associated with "motivation".

Frymier points out that motivation is an inferred construct, it can only be observed in its behavioral manifestations, its effect on other activities. Its manifestation in second-language acquisition is Carroll's "perseverance". Bloom (1968) has defined "aptitude" as the amount of time required by a learner to attain mastery—perseverance through time toward a desired behavior, certainly another manifestation of motivation.

The willingness of the learner to persevere until the acquisition of desired skills is due to his acceptance of the skill itself as important to him. Several psychologists have devoted themselves to the perception of an order in the needs of individuals. Most noted among these are Maslow (1943) and Cronbach (1963). In each of their needs hierarchies, the intellectual level—knowledge for knowledge's sake—has a low inherent priority. Unfortunately, in the American society of the Twentieth Century, second-language learning for the majority of students still remains an intellectual exercise.

Psychologists accept the proposition that some needs of the individual are characteristically acquired within cultural contexts (McDonald, p. 119). It stands that some needs are *not* characteristically acquired in a given culture. With the same native qualities, a member of one culture seems to learn a second language within a formal instructional process more readily than a member of another culture which relegates this skill to a low-need intellectual exercise.

When the need is highly evident, each can learn the second language unless the one cultural pattern has been so severely imposed as to force the learner into an avoidance-motivation strategy: aggression, withdrawal, dependency on others or a substitution of new goals. These last can often be observed in the American facing the challenge of second-language acquisition.

# Linguistics

The direct contributions of linguistic theory to foreign-language instruction is currently a topic of considerable discussion. That linguists of certain schools have had a marked influence on language materials and language pedagogy over the past twenty years is undeniable. The linguistic theories resulting from the schools of Bloomfield and Sapir saw fruit in the pedagogical work of Fries, Lado, and Brooks. Instruction in applied linguistics was an integral part of the National Defense Education Act Institute programs and has long been advocated as essential preparation for beginning teachers. A section of the Modern Language Association *Proficiency Tests for Teachers and Advanced Students* was devoted to assessing the candidate's background in linguistics.

No respectable materials production team would now omit the inclusion of a linguist. Materials widely used during the 1960's bore the unmistakable imprint of linguistic thinking. Whether or not this made them more effective is a question that may never be answered adequately, considering the McLuhan thesis that the medium itself creates behavior. This thesis is supported at the foreign-language classroom level by recent work of Politzer which indicates that is not the *type* of student activity, but the *number* of different kinds of learning situations that contributes most to foreign-language achievement.

At the same time that the descriptive school of linguistics was markedly influencing foreign-language materials and practices, the transformational-generative theory was gaining a wide number of adherents. As the decade of the 1960's closed, the transformational-generative school was undeniably the most widespread and influential movement in American linguistics.

The contributions of the transformationalists to language pedagogy are still slight. Chomsky (1966) has flatly stated that he does not believe that his theory has direct implications for second-language learning in the formal instruction process. A number of contemporary linguists who have accepted the transformational approach do not agree with Chomsky and are actively seeking ways to reconcile his theory with the instructional process. As the 1970's opened, the profession had available a number of excellent articles such as those by Fraser (1970), Scott (1970), and Spolsky (1970), addressed directly to the emerging contributions of linguistics to the instructional process.

It is safe to say that transformational theory has not as yet (1971) directly influenced classroom foreign-language instruction in a marked fashion. However, it is equally true that new foreign-language materials reflect the thinking of individuals who now view language from a transformational viewpoint. This is the beginning of an influence of transformational-generative linguistics on second-language instruction that must increase as the profession evolves.

A considerable amount of work has gone into the development of constrative programs, based upon the supposition advanced by Fries that a formal contrast between the native and target languages would enable the foreign-language educator to identify key learning problems and to determine which areas of language could be acquired most quickly. In reality, little use has been made of the contrastive grammar in materials production. It must follow, however, that future contrastive grammars will be developed around a transformational philosophy. This may either enhance or inhibit their use in the development of instructional materials, depending upon the insights, biases, and creativity of the writing team.

The actual terms used to develop descriptions of each language and the points of similarity and contrast will be colored very heavily by the linguistic orientation of the person developing the grammars. It is a safe assumption that the contrastive grammar between two languages which is constructed on a transformational model finds more in common among languages than a linguistic analysis built at the surface-phonological level.

The two main schools of linguistics are moving together despite a series of almost bitter professional encounters between proponents of each. Recent works in descriptive linguistics utilize the symbolism of the transformational school; recent works in tagmemic linguistics incorporate points of transformational theory (Cook, 1969); and the transformationalists are applying their insights to phonological analyses. This convergence appears to be fruitful and there may be implications in the resulting synthesis for the language-learning process.

More recently, Fillmore (1968) has advanced the concept of Case Grammar. Language-learning specialists should examine his theory of language performance, since it seems to more closely represent the actual linguistic attempt of an unsophisticated speaker of a second language. Fillmore posits the verb phrase as first with the balance of the sentence in the form of noun phrases which are manipulated by transformations. In contrast to the Chomskian model S—NP + VP (NP), Fillmore develops the format S—V (Agent) (Object) (Dative) (etc.). Fillmore's work is just now beginning to be known but may certainly become more developed and widely known in the 70's.

The most accepted theoretical model of language today is that of the transformational grammar approach of the mid-1960's. This is the theory as advanced by Chomsky in *Aspects of the Theory of Syntax* (1964) and presented in a simplified form by Fraser (1970). Here the (1) lexicon and the (2) semantic rules interact with the (3) base component of phrase-structure rules to produce the Deep Structure representation of language. Portions of the deep-structure representation are manipulated by the (4) transformational rules resulting in a surface-structure representation. The (5) morphophonemic rules of the language convert the abstract surface-structure representation into the phonetic form of the (6) utterance. Considerable discussion has been devoted to the actual proportion and roles that each of these components plays, particularly the concept of deep structure. It seems, however, that this model of language presents a viable concept for pedagogy, and that language-learning theorists should turn from emphasis on surface-structure manipulation toward instilling in the learner competence (in the Chomskian sense) at the deep-structure level.

The invention of a "Deep Structure Approach" on the very day that "Deep Structure died" does not necessarily mean that either theory, linguistics or pedagogy, is deficient. Subordination of one component of the grammar to another must rely upon insights gained from the native language competency of the individual.

Much thought has been given to enhancing second-language acquisition through first-language insights, and this viewpoint may be debilitating to the development of an adequate theory of second-language learning within the formal instructional framework of the education system. A "Deep Structure Approach" seems to have very viable implications for classroom instruction, especially in the light of new insights into learning theory and cognitive psychology.

This approach may very well be the formalization of what the language learner intuitively does to obtain the information about the language. A century ago, Gouin observed and built a language theory upon the seemingly intuitively but highly-structured questioning progression of a child. The language-learning approach developed by Rivenc and Guberina in France in the late 1950's exploited

Figure 6. One Simple Model of Linguistic Performance

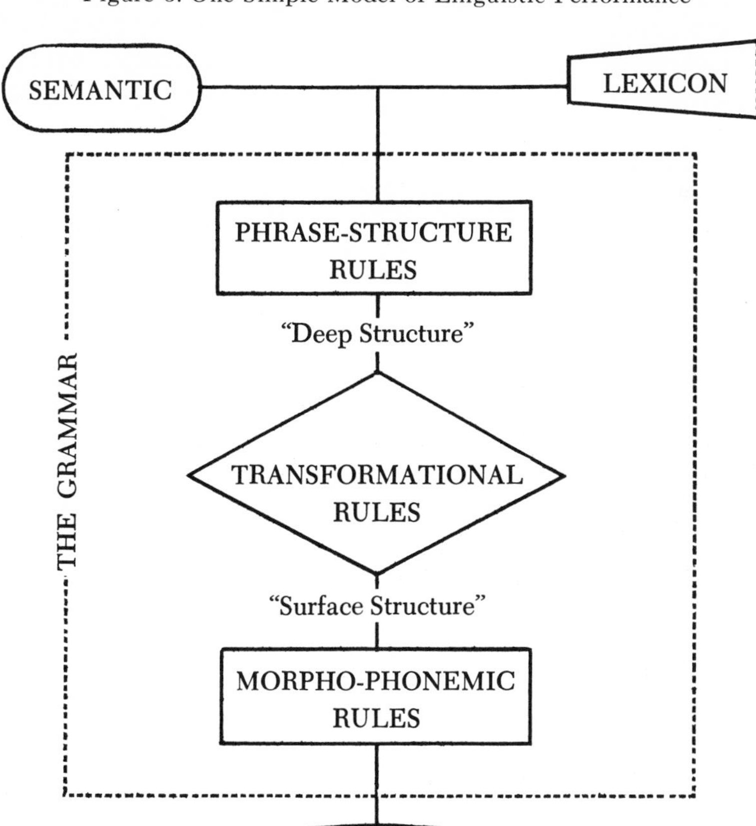


the inherent questioning technique possible in Western European languages. Through the use of highly-structured but unique questions, the learner is able to approach a novel utterance and to determine for himself exactly what role each component in the sentence plays. He is taught inductively in the Guberina-Rivenc approach to move from a phonological surface phenomenon to the underlying Deep-Structure representation. Within a short time, the learner can effectively determine not only the semantic meaning but also the structural role of each portion of an utterance that he has never encountered before (Renard and Heinle, 1969).

The structured questioning technique could also usefully be applied to Fillmore's (1968) Case Grammar model of language. Here Fillmore's Verb + (Agent) (Object) (etc.) can be paraphrased as "What is happening to whom? — where? — by whom? — how? — why?" This model seems particularly suited to the intuitive questions asked by the intelligent but linguistically-culturally naive learner in a real-life situation.

## Implications from Linguistics and Psycholinguistics

At the opening of the 70's, a number of direct implications of linguistics for classroom instruction could be seen in contemporary linguistics. The most important of these involve the linguistic objectives of instruction, the relationships of first and second languages, the development of semantic concepts, and classroom instruction.

Linguistic objectives of an instructional program are being stated in much more precise and behavioristic terms than was popular a few years ago. This is in line with the whole curricular emphasis on "Behavioral Objectives" and "Performance Contracting".

Support in terms of linguistic theory for this increased precision has been advanced by Spolsky (1970):

> "It is possible to learn enough of a language to use it in a restricted domain."
> "The functional aim of a language course must be stated specifically."

The person concerned with second-language learning must first examine the specific role that the learner is to occupy in relationship to the second language. Once this role is identified and carefully defined, the second language itself must be examined to determine the level and scope of functional mastery that the learner must control to fulfill his expected role. Finally, an active command of this amount of the language must be imparted to the learner in the most economical fashion.

Figure 7. Developing the Foreign-Language Course

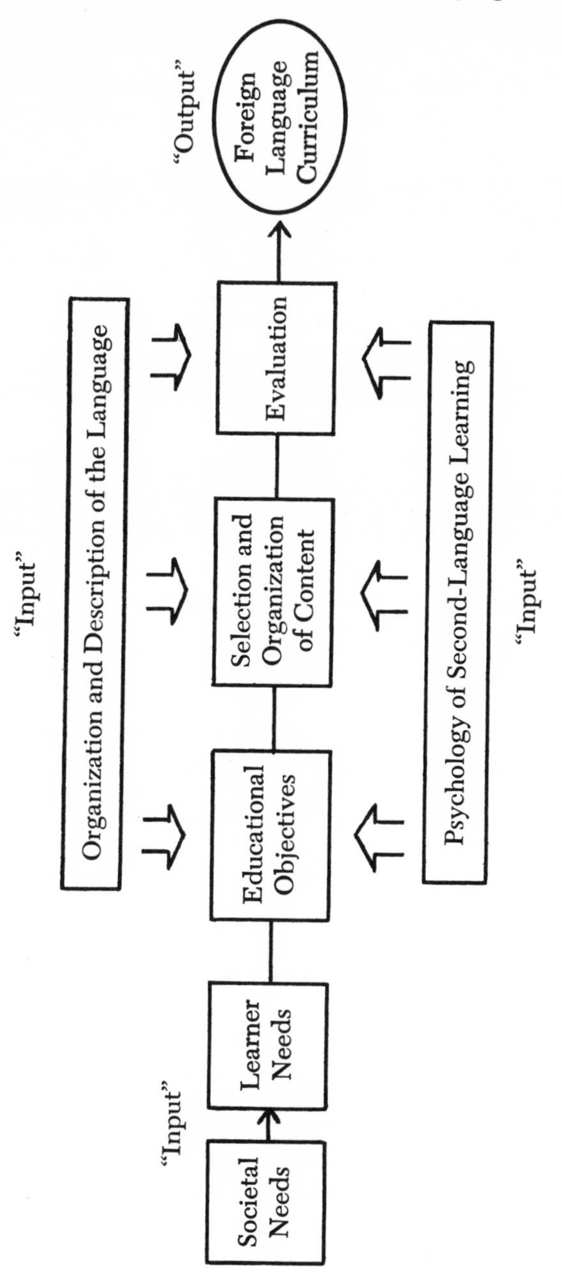

## Relationship Between First and Second Languages

The role of the native language in second-language acquisition is still one of considerable debate (Gamlin, 1968). Active use of the native language was long advocated by Sparkman (1930, 1949) and is the subject of current research (Parent and Belasco, 1970). Second-language learning is an *inferred process*—it can only be observed and its nature deduced in secondary manifestations. From observation and logical deduction, there exist relatively few real *knowns* about second-language learning.

*Language is acquired through the senses.* One can only learn that which is transmitted to the mind via the senses. In the case of second-language learning, it is obvious that the senses receive stimuli but that the mind does not necessarily perceive language. Without question, every normal human possesses a "language-acquisition device". It must be seriously questioned that a person has more than one such "input mechanism".

*Language learning is not confined to one particular spot in the brain.* One general area, perhaps, but not one particular spot. The child who has learned a language and who suffers brain damage or has a portion of the brain removed surgically will develop a new language center—the ability to do this successfully declines with age.

The behaviorist approach attempts to create in the language learner a separate mental "language center" in addition to the one used in native language performance. It is believed by some (Brooks, 1961) that the truly bi-lingual person has developed two separate language centers—*compound* bi-lingualism. The addition of a second tongue to the existing first language network was termed *coordinate* bi-lingualism.

That truly independent neural language centers do not in reality exist is readily apparent. If true, the bi-lingual would be incapable of mental translation. If true, missionary children, born and raised in a bi-lingual environment abroad, would not reflect the "foreign" language in their speech when finally brought "home" to the parental language community. A better model illustrating gradation in bi-lingualism is shown by Jakobovits (1970). This is undoubtedly a more real picture than that advanced by Brooks.

Even the truly bi-lingual person searches for words or meanings from his second language when at a loss for words or no cultural equivalent exists: ". . . and then we went to his . . . what's the word? In French it's *pension.* Oh, yes, 'boarding house'. Then we went to his boarding house and . . . ".

In terms of the realities of second-language instruction *in the school setting, compound bi-lingualism is not a practical goal* (Sparkman, 1949; Hale and Budar, 1970). Even where the program is English as a Second Language in a bi-lingual community, the school can only formalize, make explicit and reinforce what bi-lingualism students are acquiring naturally outside of class (Hale and Budar, 1970). It seems presumptuous to cling to the claim that in thirty to forty minutes per day—at ages approaching or during adolescence—a teacher can really encourage the formation of new brain centers. This is just not going to happen.

Even at the height of the acceptance of the audio-lingual approach (and the author was a strong proponent of this technique), students still made reference to the native language with *subrosa* translation, often mis-translation. The best audio-lingual teachers had to get their students past the stage of phonological interference and to combat the intrusion of English lexical items the moment students tried to be creative and deviate from the set patterns and vocabulary.

Since economy is important in second-language learning, it seems foolish to pretend that the intelligent learner is not utilizing his inherent native language mechanism to receive, perceive and categorize new language. Granted, once an adequate knowledge of the second language exists, new items can be acquired without conscious relationship to the mother tongue. However, in the thinking human, even children, the intuitive need is to know—and this, like all learning, can only be meaningful in terms of what is already known.

> "Mommy, what does *!'* mean?"
> "Psst, Joe! What does *faux pas* mean?"
> "Sir, would you define 'derivation'?"

It is possible for the intelligent learner, deposited bodily into a new culture, to learn the language. Immersion, however, is traumatic, frustrating and decidedly wasteful of the human potential. Each of us knows of the educated immigrant working at a menial job because he cannot communicate. Observe the intelligent person in this predicament, and you will find the well-worn reference grammar, the worn dictionary, and many many unfruitful digressions.

If a model of language competence is a viable construct, no matter what the particular theoretical base, then it is logical to think in terms of the second-language learner "expanding" various components of this model than to think in terms of creation of a parallel model. Lenneberg has pointed out that "man communicates in a strikingly similar pattern" (1964, p. 586). This similarity must be apparent to the second-language learner.

Gamlin (1968) summarizes his excellent discussion of the relationship between first- and second-language acquisition with the statements, ". . . second-language learning is a process which, in many ways, is different from first-language acquisition" and, "The claim that it would be possible to repeat the first-language acquisition in second-language construction is an illusion." (Stern, 1970, p. 64). Steinkrauss (1970, p. 54) offers more direct advice to second-language teachers: "You must not and cannot ignore the student's mother tongue".

# Stages in Language Learning

Second-language learning, no matter through which approach or method, follows a sequence of four basic steps: *presentation* of the item, *explanation* of the item, *repetition* to mastery, and *transfer* to appropriate real-life situations. It is in ordering, emphasis, and style of these four steps that "methods" differ. Every approach contains these either implicitly or explicitly in some arrangement, and all materials are designed to contribute to one or more of the basic steps.

*Presentation* of the item can be a variety of media ranging from hearing a word or construction in a fluent real-life speech stream to a formal listening of an item on a dictionary page. Presentation assumes *perception,* or presentation has not occurred. Good materials will provide a variety of presentation media to insure perception by individuals with varying sense-mode preferences.

*Explanation* may either precede or follow presentation: "This is the word for X" and "X means Y". It may be explicit or implicit, allowing the learner to infer meaning or generalize structural rules for himself.

*Repetition* of some sort, ranging from rote repeating to

multiple use of a structure in some type of drill activity, is an essential part of language learning. Even the best learner will repeat a new word or structure to himself, perhaps aloud or perhaps mentally, in the acquisition process. Repetition may be of the drill in rote type but seem more meaningful if it occurs within an information exchange context.

Transfer allows the learner to move from the learning situation, either structured or informal, to new situations in real-life encounters. It is the process from repetition to free transfer that constitutes the bulk of foreign-language learning material and the variety of methods devised to facilitate confidence in the learner. True transfer can never take place within textual materials but only in varying situational encounters with speakers of the target language.

*Presentation, explanation, repetition* and *transfer* (PERT) may be visualized as

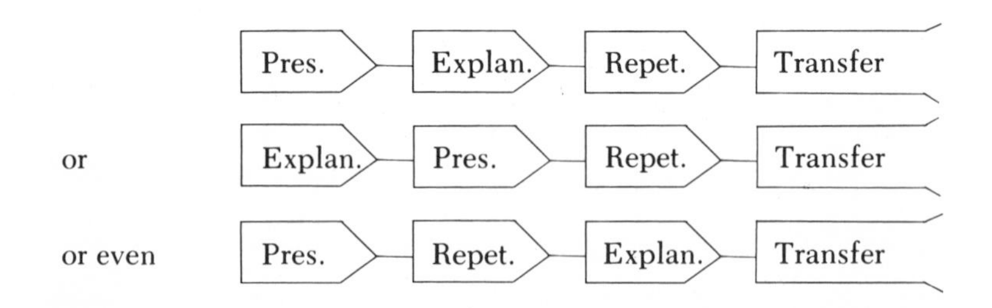


depending upon the theoretical, psychological, and linguistic bases subscribed to by the materials designer.

Disagreement is especially great among language teachers over PRESENTATION:EXPLANATION or EXPLANATION:PRESENTATION. Currently (1970) evidence is accumulating (Carroll, Chastain, P. Smith, Politzer, Harris) to support the greater effectiveness of EXPLANATION:PRESENTATION within the population of above-average intellectual abilities found in secondary schools, universities, and Peace Corps training. A compromise can be obtained by reducing the emphasis on *initial* presentation to an overview and then combining specific presentation with explanation (see Renard & Heinle, 1969). This approach will be illustrated in greater detail later.

EXPLANATION can be either by means of direct English equivalents, "acting out" by the teacher, or through specially prepared visuals. The role of the native language has, of late, been belittled but is undoubtedly preferable to ambiguity or outright misunderstanding.

REPETITION has been the *forte* of the audio-lingual approach, overdone at times and often unjustly labeled "parroting". The unfortunate fact is that rote repetition need not be—repetition of exact phrases can be elicited by the skillful teacher during a truly communicative exchange:

T. *John's sleeping.* Who is this?
S. John.
T. John. John's sleeping. What is John doing?
S. *John's (He's) sleeping.*

Note that other important interrogative techniques are at the same time acquired by the learner, even if in a passive way. These will later serve him in good stead, should he encounter new material in context with a native speaker.

Guided TRANSFER to actual free speech is the most trying task of the teacher. It challenges creativity and imagination. New vocabulary and structure can be introduced in context during this phase.

The best empiric compromise to date—and the most challenging to teacher creativity—is evident in the techniques first developed by Rivenc and Guberina and subsequently expanded and refined in this book as a "Generative Approach". In this paradigm the learner must be involved both mechanically and intellectually to language in communication—the four stages are telescopic:

In early lessons, the stages assume the relative shape and size of Part A of Figure 8. In later lessons, the emphasis understandably shifts as the learner is more fully capable of expressing himself. Examples of this will be illustrated in subsequent chapters.

It seems reasonable to expect the learner to acquire an

active knowledge of four-five items* per hour of instruction and a passive knowledge of four-five more items. Each fifth or sixth time block should be a review. This will permit a minimum active command of some 2000 items and a recognition of some 2000 more after basic instruction. This should suffice for basic communications, especially if items are carefully ordered for importance and slanted toward a specific social/occupational context.

Re-entry of items for reinforcement should be systematic until each has formally been reviewed adequately (at least five times?). It is safe to assume additional reinforcement in out-of-class communication and in oral class reviews and freely creative discussions during intensive language programs. Parameters for planning foreign-language materials should include both (1) a study of the basic procedures of language teaching; (2) empiric limitations set by the realities of the instructional process.

*Syntactic, morphological, and lexical but not phonological.

Figure 8. Stages in a "Generative Approach"

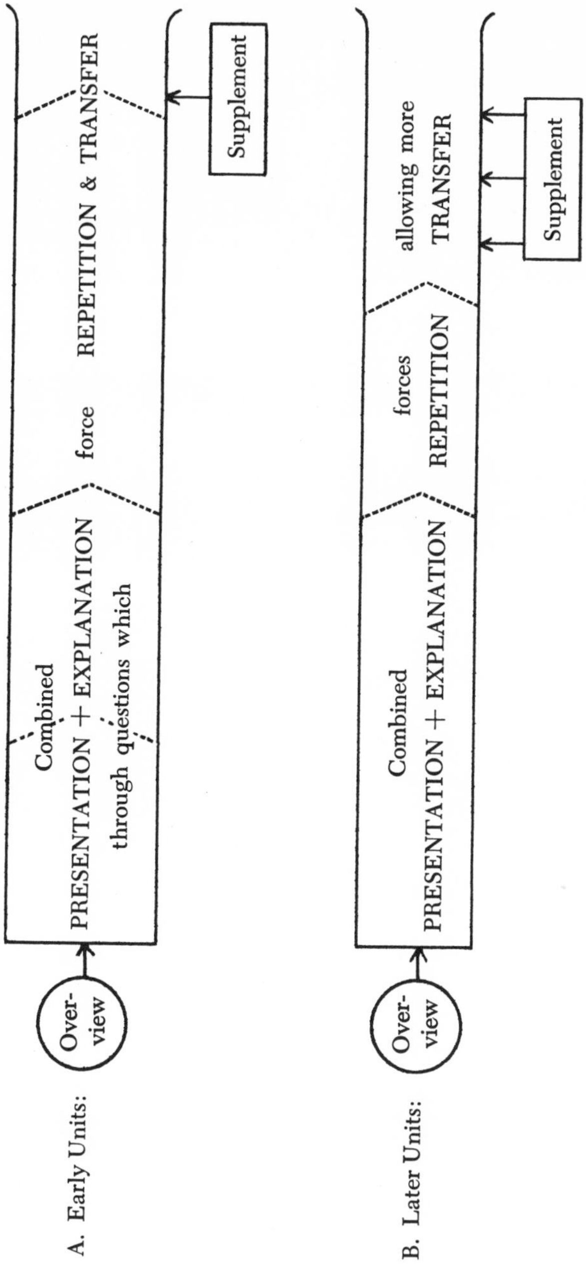

A. Early Units:
Over-view
Combined PRESENTATION + EXPLANATION through questions which
force REPETITION & TRANSFER
Supplement

B. Later Units:
Over-view
Combined PRESENTATION + EXPLANATION
forces REPETITION
allowing more TRANSFER
Supplement

# Basic Propositions for an Instructional Approach

As one moves away from the abstract and closer to the reality of actual classroom instruction, a number of "knowns" about second-language instruction can be stated. It must be clear that any "known" can only be defined in the contemporary context. The "known" of yesteryear is obviously the "false assumption" our predecessors made in the dim past of half a decade ago—or, given the publication lag—a "known" may indeed become a "myth" during the publication process itself.

Nevertheless, linguistic research, practical experience, and common sense permit the development of a limited number of "knowns" about language teaching in the formal instructional context. No claim can be made for originality of these, they are the product of the minds of John Carroll (1965) and Bernard Spolsky (1970).

Carroll's "knowns" of second language are well known but bear repeating in a time of transition in language methodology. They are quoted in abridged form as the first five "Propositions". Numbers 7 through 9 are selected from Spolsky's 1970 "Implications of Linguistic Theory for

Language Teaching". Readers should become familiar with both articles in their original form.

Carroll and Spolsky point the way toward an instructional strategy which (1) involves the student meaningfully and purposefully in the learning task, (2) utilizes a variety of presentation media and learner sensory participation; and (3) aims at a creative command of the basic syntactic features (Deep Structure) of language rather than concentrating on fluency at a more superficial stylistic level (Surface Structure). The emphasis is on conscious and creative learner involvement in communication rather than on the rote-memorization of oral patterns. The stress is on the facilitation of learning through whatever is most efficient rather than in the less efficient instillation of learner-formulated rules via over-learning of set patterns. In short, the "Propositions" call for an active learner involvement at the Deep-Structure level with the involvement of conscious thought procedure and visual as well as aural presentation of material.

Drawing upon these "Propositions", it is possible to develop some specific practical applications of psycholinguistic insights.

# Basic Propositions for Formulation of a Classroom Approach

1. "The frequency with which an item is practiced . . . is not so crucial as the frequency with which it is contrasted with other items with which it may be confused . . ." "Pattern practice drills would be improved if . . . there were constant alternation among varied patterns." (Carroll)

2. "The more meaningful the material . . . the greater the facility in learning . . ." (Carroll)

3. ". . . materials presented visually are more easily learned than materials presented aurally." (Carroll)

4. ". . . conscious attention to critical features and understanding of them will facilitate learning. . . " (Carroll)

5. "The more numerous kinds of association . . . the better are learning and retention . . . this dictates against the use of systems that employ mainly one sense modality, namely, hearing . . . " (Carroll)

6. "It is not enough to teach a language learner to respond automatically to predetermined stimuli: *language instruction must lead to creative language use in new situations."* (Spolsky)

7. *"Language can be acquired by active listening (listening and doing)* even better *than by listening and repeating."* (Spolsky)

8. "The learning of fundamental syntactic relations and processes will not be accomplished by drill based on analysis of surface structure alone." (Spolsky)

9. "Presentation of material should encourage formation of rules rather than memorization of items." (Spolsky—see also the work of Leon Jakobovits.)

# Practical Applications of Psycholinguistic Insights

A number of principles and techniques growing from structural linguistics and behaviorist psychology into the classic audio-lingual approach are now felt to be both unsupportable and inefficient (Carroll, 1955; Finocclario, 1970; Jakobovits, 1969; Spolsky, 1970). These ideas were widely accepted as truths just a few years ago (Brooks, 1960; Lado, 1964), but are no longer considered defensible. Current thinking among foreign-language educators seems to indicate that:

1. *A conscious knowledge of structure does help* the language learner to acquire a faster and more secure command of the second language. Dependency on the student's ability to deduce language generalizations from even closely controlled linguistic data can lead to inefficient learning through concentration on the wrong linguistic item or to false analogy. Focussing attention explicitly on the item followed by its use in contrastive contexts is more efficient and certainly more realistic than isolation in similar patterns.

2. *Vocabulary is of more immediate communicative im-*

*portance than structure.* Basic survival, personal welfare, and even some work needs can often be overcome with content words and pantomime alone. Learners sense this implicitly and would rather communicate haltingly and "know the words" than to acquire a greater fluency with few items. The formerly felt pre-eminence of structure and learner analogy led naturally to a concentration of few vocabulary items in tightly controlled pattern drills. This closed system would not tolerate learner creativity and became increasingly frustrating to second-language learners. The creative but guided use of the language in simulated or real situations through the use of visuals, role-playing, and direct communication is both more satisfying and more fruitful.

3. *There are many concepts* and linguistic features *common to both languages.* Often the statement has been made that there are no word-for-word equivalents from language to language. This simply is not true, especially in languages which share common cultural features. "Sleep" is probably universally translatable, "table" can be translated directly into several dozen languages and "chopsticks" is a shared concept eminently translatable from Chinese to Korean to Japanese.

4. *Functional communicative control of language is more important to a learner than over-emphasis on phonology or grammatical correctness.* Communication, even with error, is more important both intrinsically and motivationally to the learner and to his associates than fluency in a small but rigid set of language patterns. The person who can "say the most", albeit imperfectly, is the envy of a person with better pronunciation but who has nothing to say.

5. This realization leads to another, that *rote memorization of dialogues is unfruitful* and even counter-productive *when sentence structure and meaning have not been understood.* The devotion of hours to ritual chanting of dialogue lines to the point of mastery is unnecessary and stultifies learner motivation. Moreover, it can reinforce the list-learning memorization strategy that many learners uncon-

sciously employ—and which some teachers cannot refrain from employing—in language classes. Language learning is not simply a matter of learning specific sentences; it is a matter of learning the rules and processes that "generate" sentences.

Even if complete command of the exact dialogue line is considered important, it can be acquired by the learner by techniques which stress interpersonal communication and situational usage (Renard and Heinle, 1969). Mastery of the utterance should be the culmination of learning, not the beginning. By becoming a culmination, acquisition of the one utterance can permit the learner to hear, understand, and use a dozen other sentences en route.

6. Indeed, *the concept of mastery before progression is not valid.* The English-speaking child certainly is not kept from *throw* until he has overcome his /θ/ vs. / f / confusion in *three.* Nor does he not hear the passive voice until a prescribed level of maturity. The same is true of the reasoning second-language learner who can be so frustrated by being kept at a point until it is mastered that he abandons his task.

Concentration on items until mastery clearly is not necessary either for basic or for creative communication. Prater (1970) in his hierarchy of the importance of teaching phonology points out that despite current linguistic concentration on distinctive features, the phoneme is a good pedagogical concept and assigns the allophones to a less-than-necessary role in language learning. Susumu Kuno, a Japanese linguist on the faculty of Harvard University, in humorous-but-serious conversation makes the point that he speaks English with a five-vowel system. Kuno's ability to communicate at a very high intellectual level does not seem seriously impaired.

Often theoreticians stressing "mastery", although highly skilled themselves, retain marked features of a first language in their second. *What* a person has to say is more important than the forgivable errors he makes to communicate. The more realistic goal should be the *long-range shaping of skills toward mastery* while at the same time permitting, encouraging, and stimulating an expanding communicative capacity. The kind of "practice" in a foreign language that is most productive is that which involves sentence construction exercises that are motivated by a desire to communicate specific information. Far more important than repetition, recall, and meaningless manipulation drills are "real-language" exercises.

Brooks* himself recognized this in a lecture on applied linguistics in late 1966 when he stated, "We are not making native speakers out of our kids. We cannot do it; let's forget it." He then went on to point out that students should perform within the *range* of second-language phonemes and be allowed to move on to meaningful communication rather than dwelling on "native-like" pronunciation.

7. A second corollary to the realization that a conscious knowledge of the task makes learning more efficient and that there are indeed one-to-one correspondences in vocabulary and structure, is that *a complete ban on the use of the native language is not efficient.*

True, much language can be taught without reference to the native language, both vocabulary and structure, especially with the use of visuals. Ten seconds of the native language, however, can avoid ten minutes of pantomime and days or weeks of misperception. As Finocchario has recently told language teachers (1970), "We delude ourselves if we think that the student is not translating items into his native tongue." Any foreign-language supervisor, alert to student reactions and privy to the whispering in the back of the foreign-language classroom, "What's XXX mean?" must agree.

It seems only in the best interest of both student and teacher to insure that this covert translation, often highly inaccurate, be made clear from the onset. Indeed, if conscious attention is paid to important phonological or struc-

*Lecture to doctoral candidates in Foreign Language Education, Ohio State University, December 5, 1966.

tural items, semantic equivalents should be immediately made clear and relegated to second place *unless the process of semantic inquiry is the objective.*

The learner should acquire the skill of semantic inquiry, the ability to find out for himself the meanings of new linguistic units. This is an essential skill if he is to continue to grow in the language. This skill can and must be taught to the second-language learner. The prolonged and painful delusion that students will semantically "see the light" is simply not efficient and is unrealistic in most instances. Teaching him to "find the light" is a defensible but finite object.

8. Lastly, experience and reasoned judgment have indicated that *the rigid adherence to an extended audio-lingual pre-reading period is not necessary.* Interference between oral and written skills often occurs, but the problems are the same earlier or late. On the other hand, Prater—commenting on the work of Chomsky and Halle—points out that the patterning of a written language (English) may indeed *contribute* to the acquisition of phonological rules.

In any case, rapid self-directed vocabulary acquisition on the part of the learner will only come with second-language literacy. This realization has already led American foreign-language educators to reduce the suggested pre-reading phase of a popular text from ten or twelve to two weeks. The realization that half or more of American secondary (Smith, 1968) or university (Jakobovits, 1969) students prefer a course with a reading skill emphasis should make most foreign-language educators reassess objectives and procedures.

In his recent book, Jakobovits (1970) refutes the psychological assumptions of the audio-lingual approach and advances a two-factor second-language acquisition theory. There are (a) "the discovery of the underlying structure of the language by means of inductive and deductive inferences guided by (i) innate grammatical universals and (ii) simple linguistic data . . . , (b) the automatization of the phonological surface transformations of this underlying knowledge through practice". (p. 25).

Jakobovits is very careful to point out that in his theory, the automatization of speaking and understanding can only come after knowledge of the structure has been acquired by the learner through the phonological actualization of sentences the individual produces himself.

Unfortunately, Jakobovits leaves the foreign-language education in theoretical limbo, for—after showing that the audio-lingual approach is lacking and persuasively developing a new theoretical base—no effort is made to illustrate the application of this theory at the instructional level. The balance of this present work will be an attempt to relate this theoretical basis to an instructional reality via one learning strategy, a "generative" approach. It may be entirely possible for others to formulate alternative approaches to the same objective, the ability to consciously create novel linguistic utterances in a second language.

Recently, explications of the "Cognitive-Code" theory of second-language learning have been developed. This approach is still in a state of definition and flux. A "cognitive" approach may be used by one specialist to refer to a set of instructional materials which contains linguistic metalanguage, language about language, to make structure explicit and clear to the learner. Another person may use "cognitive" to refer to an instructional approach which may not include explicit structural explanations at all, but in which the learner is forced into a conscious involvement in language manipulation and production. Carroll (1965) calls it an "up-dated grammar translation approach." Chastain adopts a similar position in his writing.

Donaldson (1970), in his excellent paper "Code-Cognition Approaches to Language Learning" at the Sixth Southern Conference, points out the cognitive-code theory presents a broad base for the implementation of specific second-language programs. Going beyond this idea, one can say that within the theoretical context of conscious learner involvement there may indeed be a number of quite different instructional programs, each with different purposes, formats, and strengths.

# Language Instruction: A Generative Approach

One of the prime motivating stimuli for development of the transformational-generative theory was the inability of superficial descriptive linguistics to account for the production of ambiguous sentences. Several of these "model" ambiguous sentences have been so thoroughly discussed that they have become minor classics. Among these is the sentence which begins with:

Old men and women . . .

Separation of this phrase into its so-called Immediate Constituents presents a real problem. Does the speaker mean:

old men and (old) women . . .
*or* old men and (all) women . . .

To account for this Surface Structure ambiguity, Chomsky posited a Deep Structure which generated the Base Sentences:

old men and old women . . .
old men and all women . . .

upon which a deletion transformation can operate to remove the second adjective at the discretion of the speaker.

The role of both Deep Structure and the model of native language learning are still matters of theoretical debate. However, at least at this "ambiguous sentence" level, the linguistic behavior of the native speaker may provide some real insights toward the level of performance competency that the learner must have to operate on his own in the second language.

Suppose the "model ambiguity" does occur in the real context:

> "I'm sorry but your daughter will have to pay."
> "What do you mean? Doesn't your sign say, 'Old men and women free'?"
> "You may go on in but the lady will have to buy a ticket."
> "Look, I'm a grandfather and my daughter is forty and a woman. Doesn't your sign say *all* women admitted free?"
> "No sir, our policy is to not charge older men and older women. Her ticket will be one dollar."
> "Then why don't you say '*Old* women'? Where can I find the manager?"

Both Chomsky and the hypothetical old man know that ambiguity seldom exists long in context. Chomsky is concerned with the adequacy of a theoretical grammar, the old man with part of the price of a ticket. Not so the speaker of a language. He is more interested in removing ambiguity by establishing context. In a real-life situation, the native speaker who encounters a linguistic ambiguity or an "unknown" item intuitively questions until he can accommodate the unknown utterance.

> "Wait a minute. What's an *ick*?"
> "Smith? Was that Sam Smith or Rod Smith who was arrested?"
> "Psst! What's he talking about?"

Some speakers, of course, will tolerate unknown utterances either through fear of embarassment or lack of interest.

> "Terrific speech, Senator!" ("Didn't understand a word of it.")

"What did he say an *ick* was?"
"I dunno."

The most successful second-language learner is the one who has developed this sense of active inquiry, engaging in what Spolsky and Steinkrauss identify as "active listening". This is the learner who consciously examines the target utterance for familiar words, who does not hesitate to try to formulate sentences even if they may be wrong, and who is not afraid to ask when confronted with a new item.

"In the story this man kept his *sgian dubh* . . . "
"Excuse me. *Dubh* is black but what's a black *sgian*?"
"It's the little black knife a Scot carries in the top of his stocking. They're often used for eating. Anyhow, in the story he was all tied up and . . ."

Active inquiry is the one device that is used throughout the human life-time even if other language-acquisition facilities change biologically or psychologically:

"Mommy, what's a . . . ?"
"Honey, you use such big words."
"Do you want a 'Whippersnapper Fizz' or a 'Gin Slingshot', kid?"
"Nurse, what does 'benign' mean?"

The concept of "Deep Structure" is defined by Chomsky (1957, 1965), and summarized by Seuren (1969) as the component of the generative-transformational grammar which establishes the semantic meaning of the sentence. As Seuren states:

> "The base is the only 'creative' part of the grammar, in that the generative process starts from a general, initial symbol, which is developed into a specific (deep) structure, determining the full meaning of the sentence under generation . . . the transformational subcomponent and the semantic and phonological components are solely interpretive . . . " (p. 4).

Since the transformational component is purely stylistic, it follows that the resultant "Surface Structure" utterance can be systematically "de-transformed" by an uncomprehending listener until he reaches a point approximately at his own linguistic sophistication. In other words, the language learner with a limited command of syntax should be able—providing he is shown how—to reduce complicated native-speech utterances into more simple units which are within his linguistic repertoire. For example, simple questioning can break down a long utterance into more easily comprehensible parts.

i. "The dingbat was fizzled by the glompus in the gloaming."

If the listener only understands one or two words of the sentence, he can—and the native speaker *will*—ask the speaker to break it up for him.

ii. "Who got fizzled? and when?"

or iii. "What happened to the dingbat? and when?"

or even iv. "Who fizzled the dingbat? Oh! the glompus fizzled . . ."

This device, easily observable among native speakers, should early be a basic tool of the second-language learner, not in a secondary off-handed way but as the primary strategy to approach new linguistic material in context, opening up the language to his subsequent exploration.

It is interesting to note that generative-transformational theoreticians have not paid any formal attention to problems of discovering grammatical rules (Seuren, p. 4). This is in direct contrast with linguistics in the Bloomfieldian tradition which reached a "state-of-the-art" whereby the person approaching a new language has a definite and ordered series of steps in order to arrive at a rather comprehensive description of the language at the morphophonemic "Surface Structure" level.

O'Neill (1970), citing Bever (1970), has recently pointed out that the native speaker of a language does develop a set of hierarchically arranged strategies for establishing the grammatical relationships in sentences he hears. O'Neill points out that the second-language learner can transfer these "sentence-processing strategies" from the native language. In cases of conflicting surface details between native and target languages (English and Yoruba are cited), this transfer will be a hindrance.

O'Neill concludes his paper with the statements that (1) psycholinguistic research should detail and order these perceptual strategies in several languages and (2) that this ". . . *might* lead to a well-founded language methodology."

The profession has already gone beyond O'Neill's position by several degrees. (1) The native-speaker questioning to achieve lexical or structural clarity seems to be a language (or species) "universal." The *results*—the arrangement of the structure solicited—are language-specific. O'Neill and Bever are right, therefore, when positing the idea that the precise questions and expectations may vary from language to language. (2) As a teaching technology, it is a pedagogical approach dating at least as far back as Gouin in the 1870's. It was reoriented and formalized as a basis for the highly successful French *Voix et Images de France* materials by Rivenc and Guberina in the 1950's. (3) It seems to work not only in French but also to date in other Romance languages, Slavic languages, Hebrew and Korean.

Therefore, the native speaker's sentence processing strategy not only can be exploited but is already widely used as a technique in foreign-language pedagogy. O'Neill is wrong when he asserts that, "There is a good deal of work to be done before any of this can possibly mean anything to language teaching." (p. 7). In this case, the practitioner seems to be ahead of the theoretician. It is the thesis of this book that this is indeed a workable approach to language learning and can be reconciled to both modern pragmatic insights and linguistic theory.

The interrogative techniques formalized by Rivenc and Guberina (Renard and Heinle, 1969) working with the teaching of French provide a systematic approach to determining the semantic "meaning" and the basic structural relationships inherent in a Surface-Structure utterance. Granted, these seem superficially simple and probably work best as a pedagogical device at low levels of linguistic ability—exactly the position of most second-language learners.

It cannot be denied that it is also used by the most sophisticated of language users, "Pardon me, Lady Astorbuilt, the family jet made such an awful racket just then. Whom did you say was fizzled?"

This is the intuitive skill that must be encouraged, honed, and exploited if the learner is ever to get beyond the rudiments of a second language and to become a speaker of it. The language pedagogue must convince the learner of the viability and power of this approach in the foreign language and also convincingly demonstrate that verbal inquiry can move beyond Surface Structure to solve Deep Structure unknowns.

Indeed, this is not a new "miracle" method, but one which needs a reexamination in light of new psychological and linguistic insights.

### Hierarchy of Interrogation

There seems to be a specific hierarchy of interrogation which leads most naturally to a knowledge of the Deep-Structure arrangement of a language. A series of questions, in a definite order, can isolate the components of a sentence by function. This hierarchy is perhaps best developed in the work of Rivenc and Guberina with French. Recent applications have shown it to be applicable not only in such diverse European languages as English, Portuguese, and Russian, but also for Hebrew and Korean.

This process is described by Renard and Heinle (pp. 45-46):

> . . . each of the constituents [of a model sentence] necessitates separate treatment in the sequence of explanation questions. To signal the function of each of the elements a specific question is asked, in the appropriate sequence.
>
> The purpose of these questions is to dissociate the elements of the sound group according to "function" . . . in acts that approximate actual communication. We can generalize from this and observe that the questions used to signal grammatical function are limited in number and are re-used constantly.

The hierarchy established by Rivenc and Guberina and which seems universal to all languages is simple but powerful:

| | |
|---|---|
| 1. Subject: noun: | *What?* } is doing X? |
| proper noun: | *Who?* } |
| 2. Predicate: verb: | *What is X doing?* |
| 3. Direct object: | *What is he doing it to?* |
| 4. Indirect object: | *To whom is he* + [*verb*] + [*Direct Object*]? "To whom is he *X-ing* the *Y*?" |
| 5. Temporal | *When?* |
| 6. Locative: | *Where?* |
| 7. Qualitative: | *How?* |
| 8. Quantitative: | *How many/much?* |
| 9. Causative: | *Why?* |

As stated simply, the language learner should be in the same position as the native speaker. He should be able to always ascertain with a few simple questions, "Who is doing what to whom—and why."

Obviously, not every functional unit can be directly isolated by questioning techniques. In this case, interrogative circumlocution can be used, for example to determine an inflexional ending such as the definite past forms by contrasting with a known form:

"Does the man eat dinner now?"

"No, he *will eat* at six o'clock."

Here the functional unit serves as a minimal contrast within previously learned elements.

Using a "Generative Approach" or "Deep Structure" learner attack strategy to language—one which uses a structured questioning technique to both illuminate semantic meaning with reference to an appropriate contextual stimulus and to force acquisition through meaningful repetition in communication—it is entirely possible to quickly provide the learner with the ability to employ new linguistic items in a creative fashion. This can be clearly demonstrated with an example from a hypothetical course in "Beginning Portuguese".

The language learner has to master only two short sentences, each with an appropriate visual representation. The teacher, by using simple gestures and questions, can first force individual learners to respond with specific but meaningful utterances, can then cue and force new utterances teacher-to-student, and lastly can direct students to engage in meaningful communication among themselves.

During this process, new but logical vocabulary items can almost casually be introduced, each expanding the power of the learner's creative capacity. The reader will have to assume that the example which follows would be entirely possible in "Beginning Portuguese, Lesson II" since its English translation requires that it be illustrated here with more complicated structures—"do", for example—that are not necessary in Portuguese. Some teacher prompting will, of course, be necessary during the initial phases of learner participation.

The two short sentences to be used could include a pair such as:

1. *Eu conheço um homen que fala português.*
   (I know a man who speaks Portuguese)
   Visual: Man's head with stylized balloon indicating "speaking" with word *português.*
2. *Sua espôsa é brasileira.*
   (His wife is Brazilian)
   Visual: Woman's head and left hand on background of map of Brazil, wedding ring obvious.

With voice or tape and reference to the visual, the teacher can quickly communicate the semantic meaning:

1. "I know a man who speaks Portuguese."
   "a man" (pointing)
   "speaks" (pointing)
   "Portuguese" (pointing)
   "I know" (acts out handshaking routine with students: "I know you, you know me, him, etc."—translates quickly if necessary.)
1. "I know a man who speaks Portuguese."
2. "His wife is Brazilian."
   "His wife" (indicating man, woman, and wedding band)
   "is Brazilian" (outline Brazil on visual)

*I know a man who speaks Portuguese.*

| | |
|---|---|
| Who is this? | (It's) A man. |
| Do you know the man? | Yes, I know the man. (or: Yes, I do.) |
| Which man? | A man who speaks Portuguese. |
| Whom do you know? | I know a man who speaks Portuguese. |
| To another student: Whom does he know? | (He knows) A man who speaks Portuguese. |
| Does the man speak English? | No, the man speaks Portuguese. |
| Does he speak English? | No, he speaks Portuguese. |
| What does he speak? | He speaks Portuguese. |
| Do you know a man who speaks Portuguese? | Yes, I know a man who speaks Portuguese. |
| *His wife is Brazilian.* | |
| Who is she? | She is his wife. |
| Is he Brazilian? | No, his wife is Brazilian. |
| Who is Brazilian? | His wife is Brazilian. |
| Is she Brazilian? | Yes, she is Brazilian. |
| Does she speak Portuguese? | Yes, she is Brazilian. (or: Yes, she speaks Portuguese) |
| Do the man and his wife speak Portuguese? | Yes, they speak Portuguese. |
| Do they speak Portuguese? | Yes, they speak Portuguese. |
| Do you know a man who speaks Portuguese? | I know a man who speaks Portuguese. His wife is Brazilian. I know a Brazilian. He and his wife speak Portuguese. Brazilians speak Portuguese. |
| (with the simple introduction of *sim/não*) | I know a Brazilian man whose wife does not speak Portuguese. |

| | |
|---|---|
| | His wife speaks Portuguese but he does not. |
| Do you speak Portuguese? | No, I don't, but my wife does. She is Brazilian. |
| Is your wife Brazilian? | Yes. She speaks Portuguese. |
| Isn't he Brazilian? | Yes, he and his wife speak Portuguese. |
| (with the introduction of *bem/mal)* | |
| Tell me about Richard; does he speak Portuguese? | Yes, Richard is Brazilian. He speaks Portuguese well. His wife speaks badly. She is not Brazilian. |

Only two basic sentences—never memorized or repeated, except as part of a communicative exchange—can be exploited by the addition of a few simple expansion items in context. Coupled with previously learned items—persons of regular verbs and classroom directions, for example—the basic exchange can be *exploited* to provide for a sophisticated and meaningful verbal exchange within a relatively short time.

*Teacher:* A, ask B to find out if C and his wife speak Portuguese well.
*Student A:* B, do you know C and his wife? Do they speak Portuguese well?
*Student B:* I know C. I don't know his wife. She's Brazilian. C, do you and your wife speak Portuguese?
*Student C:* No, I speak Portuguese badly. My wife is Brazilian. She speaks Portuguese well.
*Student B:* A, C doesn't speak Portuguese. His wife speaks Portuguese well. She's Brazilian.

At this point the almost unobtrusive insertion of *americano, inglês, muito, pouco* illustrates the creative power inherent in this approach. After a creative question: response exchange, students could both *understand* and *create:*

> *"Eu conheço* um homen—êle é americano—que fala português muito bem. Sua espôsa é brasileira mais ela fala um pouquinho de inglês. Você conheçe uns brasileiros? Os americanos falam inglês muito no Brasil. Êles falam pouco português e falam mal. Você fala português muito bem."
> (I know a man—he's American—who speaks Portuguese very well. His wife is Brazilian but speaks a little English. Do you know any Brazilians? Americans speak English a lot in Brazil. They speak little Portuguese and speak badly. You speak Portuguese very well.)

This "utterance" could be within the linguistic capability of a Portuguese learner within an hour of his initial exposure to "I know a man who speaks Portuguese", without the necessity of using English and without once uttering a meaningless phrase. The feeling of involvement and the knowledge of accomplishment create in the learner the realization that he *can* learn—and is successfully learning—a foreign language.

In addition, the continued use of the interrogative to elicit an exact repetition of the key phrase has given the learner the linguistic tools to discover both meaning and structure *on his own* when faced with a novel utterance in context.

It can be clearly seen that this is a truly "Generative" approach—not in the mechanistic Chomskian definition of a Generative Grammar which symbolically describes the logic of sentence derivation—but in the larger communicative context. It is a "Generative Approach" in that each utterance is designed to *generate* in the learner an active and logical verbal response. *Language generates language* rather than repetition.

The instructional strategy just illustrated is "generative" in the Chomskian sense in that it posits the concept of Deep Structure as a viable psychological and pedagogical reality; it is "generative" in the sense that it can successfully stimulate natural language behaviors in the learner; it may be "generative" in the sense that the viewpoint of foreign-language educators is now strongly influenced by Generative-Transformational theory and therefore may reflect the biases, insights, and terminology of the school.

A *Generative Approach* to second-language instruction may indeed be descriptive. However, it may not be possible to avoid misinterpretation and misconception that may be fostered by the term "Generative Approach". Indeed, this would be most unfortunate and unfair since other more effective teaching-learning strategies may soon be developed based on the evolving Generative-Transformational Grammar theories. It does seem the most appropriate "label" to attach at this point based on the principle that *language generates language.*

# Theorectical Bases for Course Progressions

When adopting the widely accepted "systems" viewpoint for the production of instructional materials for language courses, the foreign-language educator needs to formalize the thinking and procedures utilized to develop a linear COURSE PROGRESSION which serves as the basis for subsequent materials production.

As the fundamental outline for instructional materials, the course outline must reflect both linguistic theory and pragmatic insights, combining both into the best possible marriage. At the same time, it must always be recognized that a number of biases exist and that the COURSE PROGRESSION itself will be perceived subjectively by both the author and the reader.

The transition from LANGUAGE X to a pedagogical COURSE PROGRESSION for instructional materials in LANGUAGE X seems to involve taking into account five major sources of linguistic parameters and arranging the resultant corpus into a practical teaching progression (see Figure 9). Factors which establish parameters include frequency studies of both lexical and structural items, contrastive linguistic analyses, error analyses of English-

Figure 9. Theoretical Bases for Course Progression

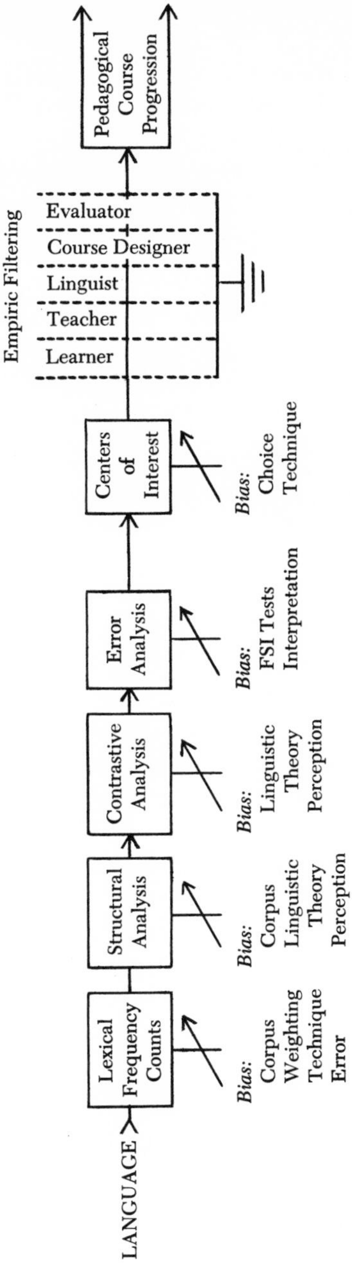

LANGUAGE
Lexical Frequency Counts
*Bias:* Corpus Weighting Technique Error
Structural Analysis
*Bias:* Corpus Linguistic Theory Perception
Contrastive Analysis
*Bias:* Linguistic Theory Perception
Error Analysis
*Bias:* FSI Tests Interpretation
Centers of Interest
*Bias:* Choice Technique
Empiric Filtering
Learner
Teacher
Linguist
Course Designer
Evaluator
Pedagogical Course Progression

speaking learners and, lastly, the actual environment in which the learner is ultimately expected to function. The body of knowledge thus defined and described, the COURSE PROGRESSION is the result of "packaging" and compromise shaped by the empirical insights gained from actual teaching-learning experiences.

Of primary importance is the LEXICAL FREQUENCY COUNT, early establishing the scope within which subsequent analysis and creative writing are to exist. Biases are introduced by the size and source of the corpus chosen, the sampling and counting techniques, the weighting assigned to various categories and human error by the speaker, transcriber, and counting program.

Of equal importance is the description of the STRUCTURE OF THE LANGUAGE. It should not only be accurate and reflect the current spoken language but should be linearly arranged to illustrate structure by order of importance in communication. Bias here can be introduced not only by the corpus but also by the theoretical orientation and the perception of the analyzing linguist.

Once adequate descriptions of both the LANGUAGE and English have been identified, a CONTRASTIVE ANALYSIS should illuminate areas of greater or lesser differences. A hierarchy of probable learning difficulty can be established, another important set of parameters for the COURSE PROGRESSION. (See Figure 9.)

An ERROR ANALYSIS of sample performances serves to illustrate and predict a hierarchy of learning problems which directly influences the COURSE PROGRESSION. These are necessarily as subjective as the sample chosen (FSI Type Interviews, for example).

The bulk of vocabulary is set by the CENTER OF INTEREST lexical analysis. This is a direction function of the social and professional context in which the learner is to function and can be biased by the technique and source used to sample vocabulary—interview, lists, materials analysis, etc.

Once the basic parameters of essential vocabulary, essential structure, ordering and supplemental vocabulary have been established, the actual arrangement must undergo an "empiric filtering" in which the realities of the learning system play a great role.

The type, motivations and expectations of the learner must be considered; experienced *teachers* can offer many practical insights into what really does and doesn't work—and in what order. The applied *linguist* can offer suggestions on transforming theory into practice. The *course designer* is concerned with the fit of the materials into a variety of curricular patterns to enhance instruction. The *evaluator* can point out areas and critical places for meaningful evaluation.

The final result, the COURSE PROGRESSION, is a deliberate compromise designed as a basis for maximally effective in-instruction but fully capable of revision and restructuring when necessary.

## Course Progression Bases—Model Peace Corps Courses

1. Lexical Counts:
   French - *Le français fondamental*
   Portuguese - Analysis of spoken Brazilian Portuguese, U. S. Naval Academy
   Korean - CCD/PC Computer Study
2. Structural Analysis:
   French - *Le français fondamental*
   Portuguese - Computer analysis of Brazilian Portuguese
   Korean - CCD/PC Computer Study
3. Contrastive Analysis:
   French - Lampach: *Contrastive French Grammar* (CAL, unpublished)
   Portuguese - Bowen and Stockwell: *Grammatical Structures of Spanish and English*
   Korean - Language Research Institute, Seoul National University: *The Grammatical Structures of Korean and English: A Contrastive Analysis.*
4. *Error Analysis* of Foreign Service Institute interviews.
5. Centers of Interest:
   Interviews, lists, technical publications.

## Criteria For Instructional Materials

After careful consideration of current theorectical insights, empiric findings, and the specific realities of second-language education in the American context, it is possible to establish tentative criteria for instructional materials. Suitable modifications will, of course, be required for the specific population and the behavioral objectives of the language program. For the framework "short-term foreign-language instruction within a formal educational setting", the following criteria seem appropriate for each instructional unit:

1. *A realistic length* which will give the learner an adequate "bite" of material for a marked move forward in linguistic sophistication but is small enough to provide him with confidence that he will finish. The learner should not be discouraged or overwhelmed, yet should also feel a sense of real accomplishment.

Units should be small enough to be "covered" in a few days' work. Longer "bites" should be subdivided in the interest of preserving good student morale.

2. *Pre-study "focus" material* which tells the learner exactly what he will learn and specifically calls his attention to pertinent structural items. This should be stated simply, clearly, and briefly.

3. *Language in context,* presented in a variety of styles: microwave, dialogue, narrative, descriptions, etc. Language in context, but language with variety—and in small enough portions to be easily acquired by the learner.

4. *A visual interface,* when appropriate, to teach both vocabulary and structure in context without intrusion of the native language as an intermediate step.

5. *The judicious use of English* when the use of visuals is inefficient or unclear. English should be used to forestall possible erroneous student translation and for structural contrasts or summaries.

6. *Language for immediate communication is most important* to the learner. He wants to be able to communicate basic needs even at the expense of fluency at the earliest stages. A command of the phonemic system precedes

allophonic refinements in a communication hierarchy. Concrete vocabulary items—content words and expressions—may be more immediately useful for halting communication than a rapid speech stream limited to a set unfruitful phrase. "Survival" vocabulary should come very early for it may be the only exposure the learner ever has to the second language.

7. *Language for creativity* is essential, direct, and immediate communication without prerequisite rote memorization of material. This assumes a teaching technique that takes only a few lines of basic instructional materials and expands them quickly and easily into dozens or even hundreds of new utterances, each a real communicative utterance. This also assumes the planned introduction of supplementary vocabulary in as great a quantity as the learner can absorb.

8. *Language for inquiry is fundamental.* The learner should early acquire basic inquiry skills to permit his active movement deeper into the language. He should quickly be able to inquire of the native speaker exactly what is being discussed, where things are, how to acquire needed objects and how to find out what he should or should not say in a given context. Active and conscious inquiry—in the language—must be an important linguistic skill early acquired by the second-language learner.

9. *Post-study formalization of structure* to permit future conscious utilization of patterns in creating new utterances. A more explicit statement of the items pointed out in the "focus", utilizing concrete examples from the instructional corpus.

10. *A rapid introduction to reading* brings the second-language learner into contact with the primary medium through which the native speaker himself continues to expand and enrich his language. The purpose of reading is more practical and immediate than to provide a contact with aesthetic language—literature. It immediately provides a vehicle for a more rapid vocabulary expansion than is possible in an oral context and permits reading for information. Truly continuing second-language learners,

even in residence, acquire most vocabulary through reading—often signs and advertisements. Literacy is the most productive language acquisition skill.

11. *Explicit cultural contrasts* which are clearly important for comfortable existence in a new socio-linguistic milieu should be clearly but concisely spelled out for the person entering the culture. "Culture in context" is a major concept but it is important that it be stated and imparted consciously. "Cultural notes", a list of "Do's" and "Don'ts", and Role-Playing situations are vehicles that are more efficient than "salting" cultural concepts into dialogue lines for future analysis.

### SUMMARY

Within these parameters, then, should the instructional materials be designed—materials which challenge, permit immediate linguistic interaction, and open the paths for learner exploitation of both what he has acquired and what he can actively acquire on his own initiative.

Jakobovits (1970, p. 21) points out that "From a theoretical point of view the development of grammatical competence should be facilitated by *getting the learner to perform* a set of transformations on families of sentences" (emphasis added), focusing on the Deep Structure rather than the Surface Structure.

Alexander Lipson has developed a strikingly similar approach for his Russian classes at Harvard University, although some features of his course are indeed unique. Lipson has demonstrated and explained his approach in a paper for Peace Corps Language (training) Coordinators (Lipson, 1970).

Lipson first teaches a corpus of Russian sentences through choral repetition, using English translation where necessary to clarify meaning. "Drawings replaced translation almost immediately and translation becomes unnecessary" (p. 1). Subsequent class work is designed ". . . to motivate members of the class to produce their own sentences with the materials of this corpus. . . . "

The basic language corpus is a series of sentences which meet the following criteria (p. 4):

1. Sentences contain examples of pertinent grammatical items;
2. Vocabulary is interesting and relevant;
3. Situations and characters are typical in tone; but
4. Atypical behavior permits verbal "playing" with the content;
5. There are alternate linguistic segments;
6. Question words are used immediately; and
7. Drawings are symbolic rather than explicit pictures—these never permit English associations.

Lipson moves from corpus acquisition into drill through the use of questions and answers. Alternate correct answers are encouraged. In this Q-A drill, Lipson forces the student to focus on the content of a sentence rather than emphasize its form. His lessons often become largely "communications drills" following a verbal puzzle situation designed to stimulate the creative thinking powers of the learner.

The reader must have already seen the similarities between the "Deep Structure" or "Generative" approach discussed in this work and Lipson's highly successful technique. Both use typical situations with a language corpus explicated by visuals followed by communication through Question-Answer situations. The "Generative Approach" utilizes this technique earlier to avoid learner acquisition of the material through choral repetition—perhaps improving upon the use of time in the classroom. It does not use Lipson's verbal "puzzles" as a basic technique but could certainly incorporate these in the transfer stages. Indeed, since Lipson *begins* a lesson with a simple verbal puzzle, largely of material he has already covered, this could easily be the culminating activity of a "Generative" lesson. It may simply depend upon where a lesson is to be divided, one may stop where another is just beginning. In any case, the "verbal puzzle" is certainly a viable technique for eliciting thoughtful communication.

One must wonder if a psychological "edge" is lost by

Lipson's beginning a new unit or work with a rehash, no matter how imaginative, of old material. This is counter to the long-established practice of permitting the student to view new material as an increment, a task to be mastered. Lipson, instead, weaves in new material in a more gradual fashion. The advantages of one arrangement over the other have not yet been tested. If one is dedicated to a "thinking man's" approach, the initial presentation of new material as an obvious task to be mastered seems more advantageous until proven otherwise.

### CRITERIA FOR A PEDAGOGICAL UNIT

Basic criteria for each pedagogical unit and its supporting references in the literature of foreign-language education include:

1. *Relevance* which results in the learner perceiving a personal need to persevere and master—Carroll (in Gage), Pimsleur, Brooks, Wight.
2. *A scientific basis* to support content—Lado, Rivenc.
3. *Minimum essential* vocabulary—*Le français fondamental,* Politzer, Brooks.
4. *New structures* introduced at the rate of four to five per instructional hour—*Le français fondamental,* Politzer, Brooks. (*N.B.* for the typical Peace Corps trainee, accustomed to a rigorous learning situation, this might be increased somewhat.)
5. Each unit of *equal difficulty*—Skinner, Lado. In addition, a variety of recent studies support . . .
6. *Intellectual involvement* of the learner, either by cognitive problem-solving (Lipson) or explicit statements about structure—Chastain, Smith, Politzer 1969, Carroll.
7. Empiric experience from a wide variety of intensive language programs (Peace Corps, VIF, private language schools, Defense Language Institute) supports the maxim, "The mind can only absorb what the seat can endure." Considering the psychological advantage gained by the learner's sense of achievement in "covering" *a number of smaller units* rather than a few larger ones, two and one-half to three hours of instruction, even with a "break"

should be ample, permitting either instruction at the rate of five-six hours (two units) per day, or eight-nine hours (three units) for "immersion".

8. More and more evidence is pointing to an individual learning "style" or "preference". If this in truth exists, it dictates a *variety of media* for the presentation of identical material. The learner can then proceed to master the target language through a presentation appropriate to his learning strategy.

9. Lastly, each unit should be *carefully planned* along the lines detailed by Banathy in order to provide the coordinator or instructor with maximum opportunity to view the specific purposes and possibilities of the unit.

Specific criteria for the pedagogical units should include:

a. a set amount of expected items for active mastery;
b. a set amount of items for passive use;
c. a variety of learning situations to keep the learner alert;
d. criterion-referenced pre- and post-tests throughout to permit need assessment;
e. structured pre-study materials.

The optimum rate of presentation of material has never been adequately determined, and undoubtedly has a wide range for various individuals. It would seem reasonable to assume that *one new item* can be introduced in an intensive small class situation at the average rate of *one every five minutes.* This can be altered and adjusted through experience gained in field testing. At this rate one could expect a language learner to be familiar with as many as 4000 items by end-of-training, a competence approaching native-like ability in common situations.

# Practical Pedagogical Unit

Placing the Presentation: Explanation: Repetition: Transfer stages within the parameters established by the basic criteria produces a practical pedagogical unit: initial rapid over-view, detailed presentation-explanation, repetition, and transfer in combination with previously learned material. These stages seem more pedagogically efficient if they blend together. Detailed steps would then include:

1. Initial over-view presentation to illustrate unity of a two-three or five-six hour segment.
2. Specific *presentation* and *explanation* of material containing 8-10 new structural items. *Explanation* may involve the initial stages of *repetition,* presenting an opportunity for instructional economy.
3. Repetition of new structure in *combination* with previously mastered material can blend into limited *transfer.*
4. This material then becomes "previously learned material" as it is blended into a new PERT phase in an on-going cumulative process.

Actually each phase should be written to culminate in a brief evaluation activity which will determine the ability of the learner to progress. This can actually be informal but is

Figure 10. Block Diagram of a Sample Pedagogical Unit

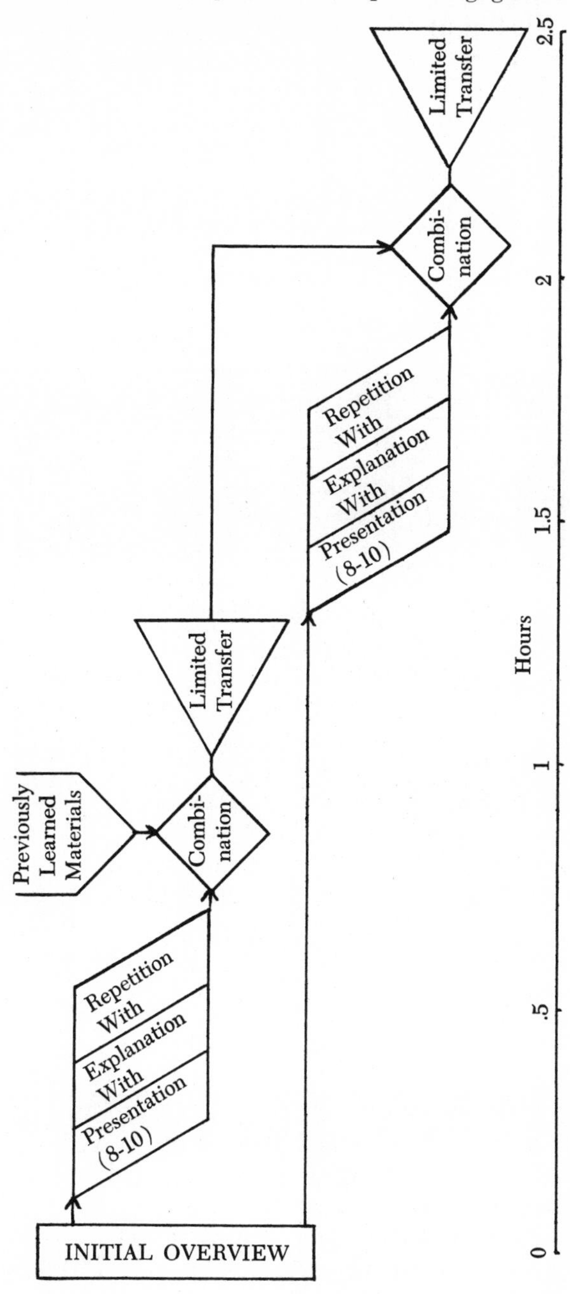

important to effective progress. Should the assessment indicate non-acquisition of the material, alternate media must be provided to permit reinstruction until adequate control is gained.

Figure 11.

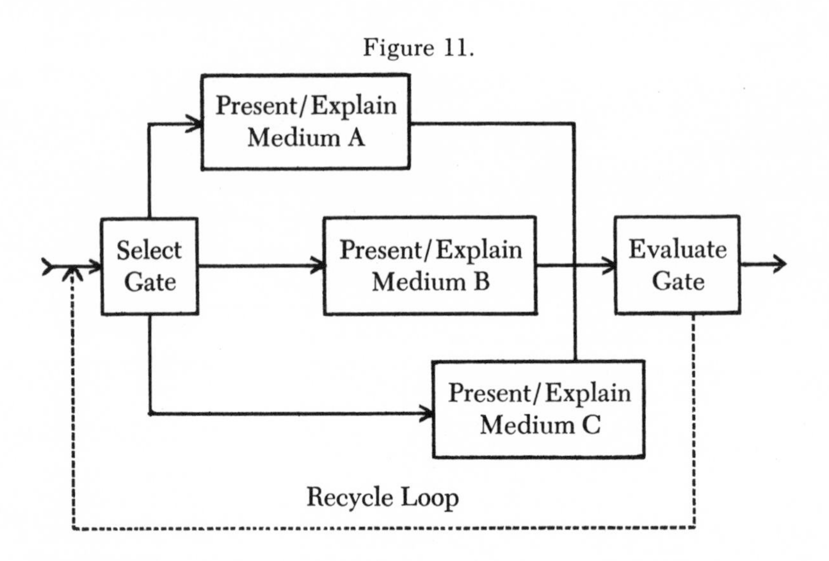


For immediate course development purposes, planners should concentrate on a linear progression of materials (one medium) with alternate media developed after the initial core. An outline of this format for Portuguese was described in Volume 1 of the Newsletter *Individualization of Foreign Language Learning in America.*

Since the initial linear course (medium "A", for example) is to be basic instruction for all types of individuals, a multi-sensory approach is directed for maximum effectiveness. This should involve explicit statements where necessary to achieve parsimony of time/effort and as many sense perceptors as possible—audio, lingual, visual, kinesic, and tactile as well as intellectual.

## Sample Pedagogical Units

Incorporating the criteria suggested into a proposed pedagogical unit will result in a progression of activities as outlined below. "Passive" materials are intended for the learner to read for content or reference; "Active" implies involvement in *active* listening, speaking, reading, writing, and manipulation. Most "passive" material, the linguistic corpus, and formal statements should be included in a *Basic Text* while "active" student material may include classwork or a *Workbook Kit* which includes audio stimuli but will rely for its main strength on the verbal exchange of the classroom—meaningful but guided conscious use of language in live communication.

### Outline of Sample Unit

| | | |
|---|---|---|
| I. | "Focus": | |
| | a. Statement of Purpose | (Passive) |
| | b. Pre-test (if appropriate) | (Active) |
| II. | Linguistic Corpus: | |
| | audio, audio-visual, graphic | (Active) |
| III. | English Equivalents (if necessary) | (Passive) |
| IV. | Manipulation: | |
| | suggested types of activities, exercises | (Active) |
| V. | Formalization: | |
| | a. Structural Notes | (Passive) |
| | b. Cultural Notes | (Passive) |
| VI. | Expansion: | |
| | a. incorporation of earlier material | (Active) |
| | b. supplementary vocabulary | (Active) |
| | c. supplementary structure | (Active) |
| VII. | Communication: | |
| | a. role-playing | (Active) |
| | b. narration | (Active) |
| | c. description, etc. | (Active) |
| VIII. | Cultural Notes | (Passive) |
| IX. | Evaluation | (Active) |
| N.B. | Each step should have a built-in evaluative component before a final summary phase. | |

An example of how this outline could actually be implemented is detailed in the balance of this chapter. Since use of the foreign language will perhaps mask the meaning or the purpose of language activities, English translations are included in brackets [ ] for the convenience of the reader. Please remember that these would *not appear* in the actual text.

The illustrative material is adapted from the first unit of BRAZILIAN PORTUGUESE, an audio-visual course developed for the Peace Corps by Maria Chapira. Comments and pedagogical notes for the reader-teacher are provided in the text. These are again bracketed [ ] as they would not appear in the texts intended for student use. Parentheses ( ) *would* appear for the learner's illumination and guidance.

Unidade 1 - APRESENTAÇÃO

PURPOSE: . . . to permit you to identify yourself and others; to exchange common greetings; to practice the new sounds of Portuguese; and to become familiar with some basic points of Portuguese grammar that differ from English.

Therefore,

FOCUS ON . . .

1. Forms of the verb of "identity" *ser: é, sou;*
2. the nasal sounds of Jo*ão,* n*ão,* b*om* and s*im;*
3. sound changes on the ends of verbs: conh*ece,* conh*eço;*
4. sound changes on the ends of adjectives: brasileir*o,* brasileir*a;*
5. common use of the double negative: Não conheço, não.

[PEDAGOGICAL NOTE: This material could be placed on an individual home-study cassette to permit the learner to *hear* what he will be actively *listening* for in class.]

APRESENTAÇÃO

[Note: Each numbered line is accompanied by a visual which serves as to convey semantic and/or structural concepts.]

1. Apresentador: Êste é João.
   [This is John]
2. Apresentador: Bom dia, João.
   [Good day, John]
3. João: Bom dia.
   [Good day]
4. Apresentador: Você é João?
   [You're John?]
5. João: Sou sim.
   [Yes, I am]
6. Apresentador: Esta é Rita.
   [This is Rita]
7. Apresentador: Rita, você conhece João?
   [Rita, do you know John?]
8. Rita: Não conheço não.
   [No. I don't know (him)]
9. Apresentador: João, apresento Rita.
   [John, I introduce Rita]
10. João: Muito prazer, Rita.
    [Glad to meet you, Rita]
11. Rita: Muito prazer, João.
    [Glad to meet you, John]
12. Apresentador: João é brasileiro.
    [John is Brazilian]
13. Apresentador: Êle é estudante.
    [He is a student]
14. Apresentador: Rita é brasileira.
    [Rita is Brazilian]
15. Apresentador: Ela é professôra.
    [She is a teacher]

[PEDAGOGICAL NOTES:
The unit should be presented to the class in the following fashion:
1. A quick "one-time through" overview of the material, visual and audio. The visual images should appear *before* the accompanying line of Portuguese.
2. Each of four segments is then taught independently

with the use of visuals and simple questions based upon the LANGUAGE IN CONTEXT.

a. Presentation of each line;
  b. Explanation of meaning by pointing, questioning and a word of English if necessary;
  c. Repetition of each line forced by teacher questioning:
    T. *Êste é João.* Quem é?
    S. João / é João.
    T. Quem é êste?
    S. *Êste é João.*
  d. Transfer by involving the class in interpersonal communication:
    T. Quem é êste?
    S1. Êste é Paulo.
    T. Pergunte a Paulo: Quem é esta?
      (prompt until student says. . . )
    S1. Paulo. Quem é esta?
      (and S2 replies. . . )
    S2. Esta é Maria.]

**SEGMENT A**

1. Apresentador: Êste é João.
2. Apresentador: Bom dia, João.
3. João: Bom dia.
4. Apresentador: Você é João?
5. João: Sou sim.

LANGUAGE IN CONTEXT . . .

| | |
|---|---|
| Quem?<br>Boa tarde.<br>Boa noite.<br>É sim.<br>Eu sou ______.<br>Personal Names<br>É | (Note: It is the responsibility of the teacher to integrate these items into the communicative process.) |

[PEDAGOGICAL NOTE: By the end of the transfer phase of this Segment, exchanges of this type should be within the repertoire of all students:

| | |
|---|---|
| Quem é êste? | |
| | Êste é Paulo. |
| E você? Quem é? | |
| | Sou Maria. |
| Você é Maria? | |
| | Sou sim. |
| Bom dia, Maria. Pergunte a Paulo, Quem é êste? | |
| | Paulo, quem é êste? etc.] |

**STRUCTURAL NOTES**

1. How to make questions:
   Portuguese, like English, makes a question from a simple statement by raising the voice at the end of the sentence.
   You're John. You're John?
   Você é João. Você é João?
2. "Identity" between two items in a sentence is expressed by the forms of the verb *ser*:
   Você é João? Sou, sim (João).
   You = John? Yes, I = (John)
3. Notice how verbs change to *reflect* their pronoun:
   você + /ser /——→voc*ê* *é*
   eu + / ser /——→e*u* so*u*
4. *bom* and *boa* are alternating forms dependent upon the word they describe. This is very common in Portuguese and will become familiar before the end of this unit:
   bom dia
   boa tarde
   boa noite

**SEGMENT B**

5. Apresentador: Esta é Rita.
6. Apresentador: Rita, você conhece João?
7. Rita: Não conheço, não.

[PEDAGOGICAL NOTE:The teacher will continue to actively use the contrast *êste/esta* and continue free communication until students are able to engage in exchanges like the example below. Negatives should be used with the index finger.

T. Maria, você conhece João?
S1. Não conheço/não.
T. Quem você conhece?
S1. Conheço Paulo.]

**STRUCTURAL NOTES**

1. Notice the continued reflection of the pronoun in the verb:

    você + / conhecer / ⟶ voc*ê* conhec*e*
    eu + / conhecer / ⟶ (e*u*) conheç*o*

    If you were to come across new Portuguese verbs with the same sound ending as the one you now know, would you make the correct change to reflect the personal pronouns? Try it.

    conhec*er* ⟶ eu conheç*o*
    você conhec*e*

com*er* (to eat) ⟶ eu com __
você com __
escrever (to write) ⟶ eu escrev __
você escrev __

| RULE: For verbs that end in *-er*: |
| --- |
| *-er* ⟶ *-o* for *eu* |
| *-er* ⟶ -e for *você* |

2. Portuguese "Yes" follows the verb in contrast to English:

| | |
| --- | --- |
| Yes, I am | Sou, *sim* |
| Yes, I know (him) | Conheço, *sim* |

3. Double negatives are the most common Portuguese form. "No", *não,* by itself is unnatural and is most often accompanied by the verb form.

Não conheço
or. . . .*Não* conheço *não*

This arrangement does *not* usually occur in the affirmative:

Sou, *sim*
but . . . .*Não* sou, *não.*
Conhece, *sim*
but . . . .*Não* conhece, *não.*

**SEGMENT C**

"Introducing Ritual"

9. Apresentador: João, apresento Rita.
10. João: Muito prazer, Rita.
11. Rita: Muito prazer, João.

People shake hands and use the stock phrase *muito prazer* when being introduced. Who is doing the introducing? The *apresentador* (narrator) is speaking about something he himself is doing so he is using the 1st person form, "I".

João, (e*u*) apresent*o* Rita.

[PEDAGOGICAL NOTE: Teacher and members of the class will introduce one another, continuing the ritual with already learned material in exchanges like:

T. Paulo, você conhece Maria? (use finger with negative)
P. Não conheço, não.
T. Paulo, apresento Maria.
P. Muito prazer, Maria.
M. Muito prazer, Paulo.
T. Agora, Paulo, você conhece Maria?
P. Conheço sim.]

**SEGMENT D**

12. Apresentador: João é brasileiro.
13. Êle é estudante.
14. Rita é brasileira.
15. Ela é professôra.

PRE-STUDY . . . LANGUAGE IN CONTEXT

Pay close attention as your teacher will introduce the following new forms in spoken Portuguese:

Os Estados Unidos . . . . . . . . . *the United States*
americano
nós somos . . . . . . . . . . . . . . . . . *we are*
êles são . . . . . . . . . . . . . . . . . . . *they are*
É! . . . . . . . . . . . . . . . . . . . . . . . *That's it!*
The plural forms: brasileir*os*, american*os*

[PEDAGOGICAL NOTE: The teacher will present the segment audio-visually before using gestures and the blackboard to introduce supplementary vocabulary. The class should shortly be able to handle exchanges such as:
T . Você conhece Maria?
S1. Conheço sim.
T . Maria é brasileira ou americana?
S1. Ela é brasileira.
T . É sim!]

GENDER—Most languages have several ways of "sorting" words. One common "sort" is by arbitrarily assigning a gender or a sex to everything. English has lost most of this but retains traces as we refer to things dear (i.e., ships) as "she", or in "Look out! Here she comes!"

All Portuguese nouns are assigned a gender, masculine or feminine, usually marked by the ending *-o* or *-a*. Plurals, like English, usually are formed by adding *-s*.

| MODEL: | | Masculine | Feminine |
|---|---|---|---|
| | singular: | o brasileiro | a brasileira |
| | plural: | os brasileiros | as brasileiras |

Notice that *both* the noun and its article must be the same (agree) in gender and number.

*o* brasileir*o* + [plural] ⟶ *os* brasileir*os*

*a* brasileir*as* + [plural] ⟶ *as* brasileir*as*

INVITATION . . . Following the model,

o americano + [pl.] becomes ⟶ ? american ?
a americana + [pl.] ⟶ ? american ?
o mexicano + [pl.] ⟶ ? mexican ?
a mexicanas + [pl.] ⟶ ? mexican ?
Ela + [pl.] ⟶ Ela ?

Words ending in *-e* simply add *-s* to form the plural:

êle + [pl.] ⟶ êl*es*
você + [pl.] ⟶ voc*ês*

Words ending in most consonants add *-es*:

senhor + [pl.] ⟶ senhor*es*
professor + [pl.] ⟶ professor*es*

*Cultural Note:* Portuguese speakers tend to use politeness in their speech more than Americans, addressing adults they don't know well as "sir" or "ma'am," *o senhor* or *a senhora.* A question like, "O senhor é americano?" can mean, "Is the gentleman an American?" but can also mean, "Are *you* an American?"

SUMMARY: The Personal (Subject) Pronouns, common forms

| | Singular | Plural |
|---|---|---|
| speaker | eu | nós |
| spoken to | você | vocês |
| spoken about | êle, ela | êles, elas |
| Polite (indirect) | o senhor | os senhores |
| | a senhora | as senhoras |

SUMMARY: Simple Portuguese SENTENCES take the form . . .

| (Subject) | (predicate) | (object *or* complement) |
|---|---|---|
| Noun Phrase - NP + | Verb – V + | Noun Phrase – NP |
| Rita | é | brasileira |
| Você | é | americano |
| Eu | sou | professor |

INVITATION: Try fitting other sentences you can already say to the Sentence formula. Some words are already done as cues for you.

| Sentence becomes | | NP | + | V | + | NP | |
|---|---|---|---|---|---|---|---|
| | 1. | Rita | | é | | brasileira | . |
| | 2. | ____ | | sou | | ________ | . |
| | 3. | Você | | ____ | | ________ | . |
| | 4. | ____ | | ____ | | americanos | . |
| | 5. | Nós | | ____ | | ________ | . |
| | 6. | ____ | | são | | ________ | . |

SUMMARY: Forms of the "equating" verb SER

| | | | |
|---|---|---|---|
| (speaker) | 1. Eu | sou | |
| (spoken to) | 2. Você, o Senhor | é | Singular |
| (spoken about) | 3. Êle, ela | é | |
| (speaker) | 1. Nós | somos | |
| (spoken to) | 2. Vocês, os Senhores | são | Plural |
| (spoken about) | 3. Êles, elas | são | |

Impersonal: É! É? Não é? (Né)?

INVITATION: You can now create sentences using forms of SER (=)

| NP | = | NP |
|---|---|---|
| eu | = | americano |
| vocês | = | brasileiros |
| êle | = | estudante |
| os senhores | = | professores |
| nós | = | estudantes |

or with the negative não + SER (≠), "does not equal":

| | | |
|---|---|---|
| êles | ≠ | ___?___ |
| você | ≠ | ___?___ |
| eu | ≠ | ___?___ |
| nós | ≠ | ___?___ |

And finally, can you make these symbols into spoken Portuguese questions and answers?

| | |
|---|---|
| =? | =! |
| ≠? | =! |
| =? | ≠! |
| ≠? | =! |

LANGUAGE IN CONTEXT: Ritual Greeting . . .

| | |
|---|---|
| Como vai? | *How are (go) you?* |
| Vou bem, obrigado. | *Fine, thanks.* |
| E você? | *And you?* |
| Vou bem, obrigado. | *Fine, thank you.* |

[PEDAGOGICAL NOTE: Following the teacher-directed introduction of this final ritual, teacher and students should finish Unit I with verbal exchanges of the following complexity, aided by visuals and gestures where necessary:

-Bom dia. Como vai?
-Vou bem, obrigado. E você?
-Vou bem, obrigado. Você conhece a Rita?
-Não conheço, não.
-Rita é professôra. Rita, apresento Paulo.
-Muito prazer, Rita.
-Muito prazer, Paulo. Você é americano, não é?
-Sou, sim.]

PARA LER (For Reading). . . .

Maria e João são brasileiros. Maria não conhece Paulo. Paulo é americano. João apresenta Maria a Paulo.

João: Maria, apresento Paulo.
Maria: Muito prazer, Paulo.
Paulo: Muito prazer, Maria. A senhora é brasileira?
Maria: Sou sim. Sou professôra de português.

João: Paulo, você é dos Estados Unidos, não é?
Paulo: Sou, sim. Sou americano. Você é professor?
João: Não sou, não. Sou estudante.
E*u* estud*o* português.

**THINGS TO FIND OUT . . . .**

a. Who speaks Portuguese—and where?

b. Are there more people in South America who speak Spanish or Portuguese? (Clue: On what continent is Mexico?)

c. In terms of numbers of speakers, how do the major Western European languages rank? (English, French, German, Italian, Spanish, Portuguese.)

d. Is Spanish different from Portuguese?

e. How different are they?

f. Is Portuguese spoken differently in different places?

g. Where did Columbus go to study for his famous voyages of exploration?

h. Where does the name Brazil come from?

i. Which Europeans first explored trade routes to Africa and India?

---

**POST SCRIPT**

By the time the class has progressed through the sample unit illustrated—probably before three hours of instruction—they will have a "communications command" of limited but important Portuguese. The class repertoire would be sizeable and the foundations have been laid for considerable future structure.

The class is aware of the necessity for careful, conscious attention to spoken Portuguese, particularly for the key final sounds that signal person, gender, and tense. The symbols used will gradually permit economy as the student becomes familiar with them.

Despite the deceptively simple initial material, there is considerable "meat" to this unit. The student has learned the important copula verb SER and two forms of the irregular verb IR which will quickly be used to make the immediate future tense ("I'm going to eat"). The concept of verb conjugation has been implanted and that of gender, number, and agreement made explicit. These will be continued and exploited in future units.

In summary, after several hours of class work the student has learned a great deal, both in the ability to create and utter meaningful sentences and in the conscious knowledge of what he is doing. This has occurred ***without*** "meaningless repetition" of words or phrases. No utterance need be made by the learned except in a truly communicative encounter.

## DIALOGUE AFRICAIN CONTEMPORAIN

The illustrative *Brazilian Portuguese* unit shows what can be done with the very first language lesson. More perspective can be gained by examining a slightly later unit following the same general format in another language, French.

*Dialogue Africain Contemporain** is a basic French course developed by a team under the direction of Lee Sparkman and the author to train Peace Corps Volunteers destined for service in West Africa. It is available to schools and universities under agreement with the Peace Corps. Portions of Unit IV, "Une visite," of this text are reproduced to illustrate how a "real" unit in an audio-visual course using a "Deep Structure" of "Generative" approach appears in student format. For economy, only the beginning (lines 1-10) and the end (lines 33-40) of the *Sketch* and Part B (lines 10-21) of the *Mécanisme* are reproduced.

Although "Une visite" is largely self-explanatory, please note that visuals accompanying each line of material have been seen by the class in color filmstrip form for an hour or more in active language "give and take." The size and clarity of visuals are reduced, but this is by design since

*The Center for Curriculum Development, Inc., Philadelphia, Pa.

they are not intended to illustrate the text but only to serve as a "prompting cue" to the student during individual study.

The reader should also note that suggested activities which are peculiar to a Peace Corps training situation are replaced with more appropriate activities for the school edition. The author's comments again appear in brackets [ ] and are not a part of the original text.

### Notes to Students

1. *In Unit IV you will learn the following:*
    1) how to make a sentence negative (e.g., It's not a large compound);
    2) how to say something is very . . . (e.g., very dark);
    3) how to ask if someone is at home;
    4) how to ask how many things there are in something;
    5) more expressions of location;
    6) more descriptive adjectives;
    7) how to report what someone else said (e.g., Seydou says that she is there; They ask if the teacher is in class);
    8) a number of new words indicating action;
    9) how to use the verbs you already know in the third person plural (e.g., They enter the room);
    10) the second person singular (familiar) subject pronoun and corresponding verb form.

2. *You will study the following points of grammar:*
    1) use of the negative *ne . . . pas*;
    2) adverbs that modify adjectives—*très* +. . . ;
    3) coordination of NP complements—*le X de . . .et de . . .* ;
    4) the second person singular subject pronoun (*tu*), and the corresponding forms of *être, avoir,* and regular *-er* verbs;
    5) the familiar form of the imperative (commands);
    6) third person plural verb forms;
    7) verb phrases that contain no complement;

8) verb phrases that contain a direct object complement;
9) verb phrases that contain an indirect object complement;
10) verb phrases that contain both direct and indirect objects;
11) verb phrases that contain prepositional-phrase complements;
12) indirect discourse (*répondre que . . .* , *demander si . . .*);
13) the question word *Combien de . . .* ? (How many . . .?)

3. *Things to do.*
   1) Find out what a typical *concession* would look like and make a drawing or scale model.
   2) Find out where in the *concession* various daily activities are carried out: where people sleep, bathe, dress, eat, work, play, relax, etc.
   3) Find out about the division of labor in a *concession*: which work is performed by men, which by women, which could be done by either sex, and how work is divided within one sex, e.g., how women in a *concession* divide the work.
   4) Find out about the games children play—what they play with, where they play, how closely they are supervised, etc.
   5) You have gone to visit a public school in the country to which you have been assigned. The teacher and the students ask you to tell them about life in the United States—how people live, what they live in, where they live, etc.

---

[PEDAGOGICAL NOTE: The Sketch contains the basic new material to be learned in this unit. For economy's sake, only selected lines of the forty of "Une visite" are shown, the first ten and the final few lines.]

CCD/PC French
DAC-Dialogue Africain Contemporain

Unit IV
Page 1

SKETCH
UNE VISITE.

1 VOIX:
- Voilà Miata.

2 C'est une amie de Daro.

3 Daro arrive au village.

4 Elle entre dans la concession.

5 Seydou, le mari de Miata, est dans la cour.

A.

6 Daro parle à Seydou.

7 DARO:
- Bonjour, Monsieur.
SEYDOU:
- Bonjour, Madame.

8 DARO:
- Je suis une amie de Miata.

9 Est-ce qu'elle est chez elle?

10 

VOIX:
- Seydou répond qu'elle est là.

---

CCD/PC French
DAC-Dialogue Africain Contemporain

Unit IV
Page 4

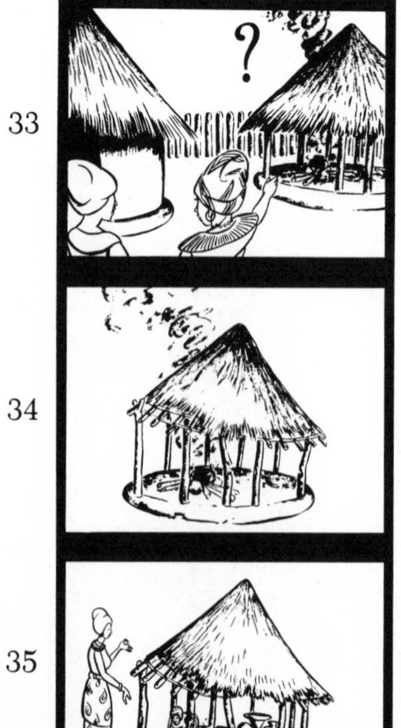


33 DARO:
- A côté, c'est la cuisine?

34 MIATA:
- Oui; elle est vieille.

35 DARO:
- Elle est bien rangée.

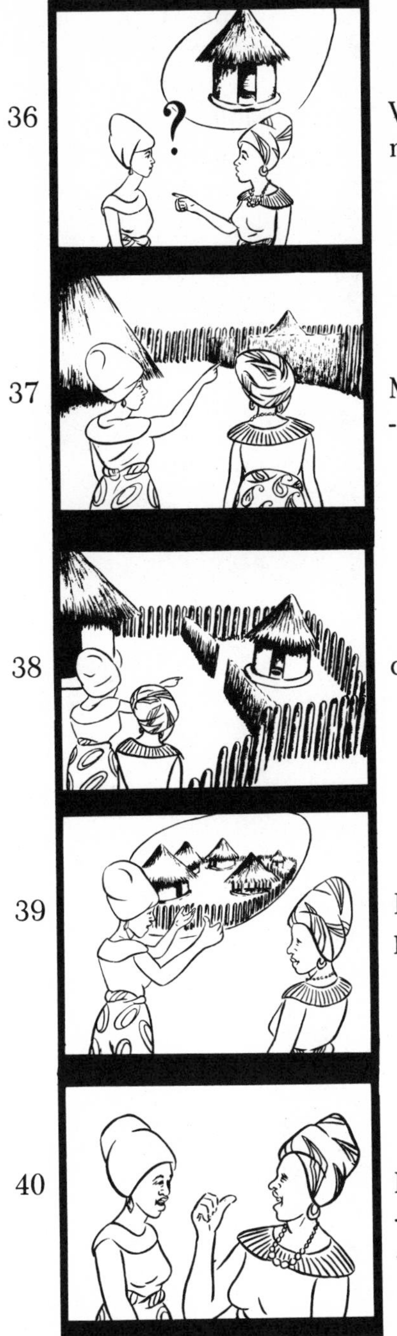

36 Vous avez les W.C., n'est-ce pas?

**D.**

37 MIATA:
- Oui, ils sont là-bas,

38 derrière la clôture.

39 Est-ce que la maison te plaît?

40 Daro:
- Oui, elle me plaît beaucoup.

[PEDAGOGICAL NOTE: The *Mécanisme* is a "mini" corpus designed to introduce with emphasis a particular structure. It may be as long as the *Sketch* but its segments do not necessarily have to have internal cohesion; they may be entirely unrelated. In "Une visite" all four segments have to do with taking Aya to school. Considerable culture can also be imparted in the *Mécanisme*, and it is a good vehicle for the introduction of additional vocabulary in context. Segment B is illustrated.]

CCD/PC French
DAC-Dialogue Africain Contemporain

Unit IV
Page 6

12 ALPHA:
- Awa rentre chez elle;

13 Les élèves entrent dans la salle de classe.

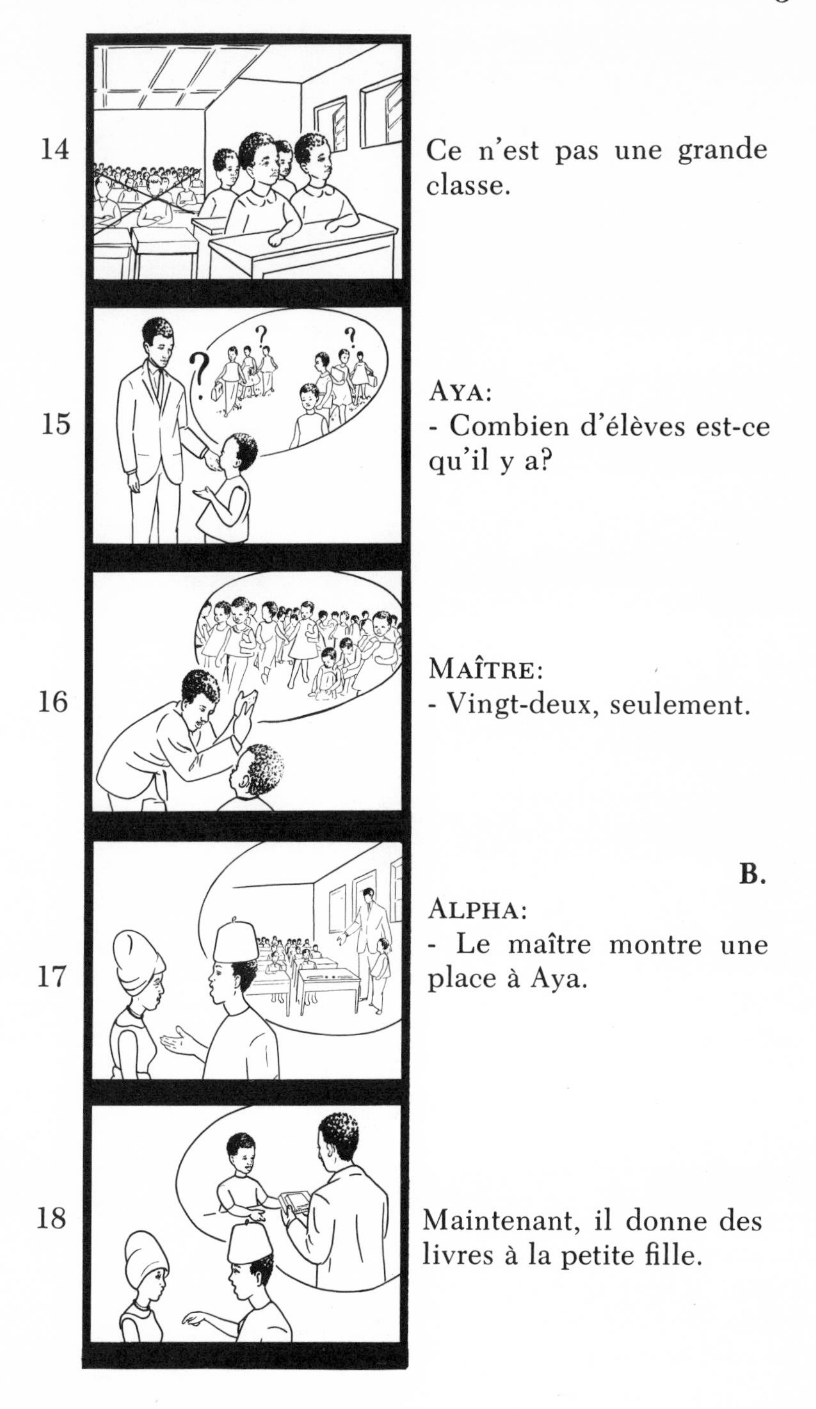

14 Ce n'est pas une grande classe.

15 AYA:
- Combien d'élèves est-ce qu'il y a?

16 MAÎTRE:
- Vingt-deux, seulement.

**B.**

17 ALPHA:
- Le maître montre une place à Aya.

18 Maintenant, il donne des livres à la petite fille.

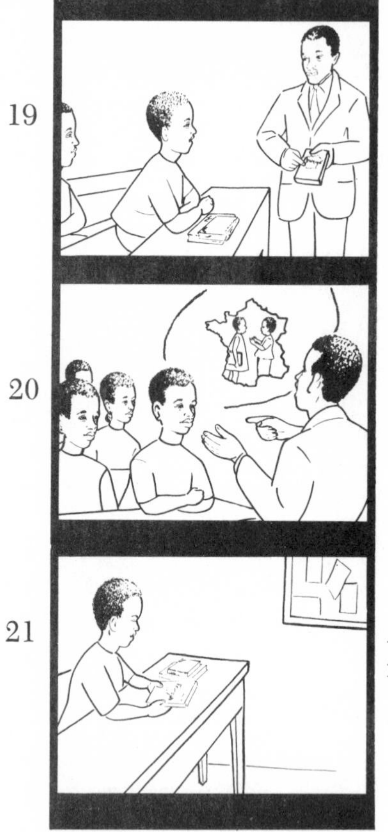

19 Il montre à Aya le livre de français.

20 Il demande aux élèves si elles parlent français.

21 Aya regarde son livre de français.

---

CCD/PC French — Unit IV
DAC-Dialogue Africain Contemporain — Page 9

## Cultural Notes

### I. Polygamy

According to some estimates 1/4 to 1/3 of married West-African non-Christian males have more than one wife.

While traditional law does not set any limit on the number of wives a man can have, Moslem law sets it at four.

Before taking a second wife, a man consults his first wife and seeks her approval of the second wife. He builds a new *case* and thereafter divides his time impartially between the *case* of the first wife and that of the second.

## II. Child Rearing

Very young children stay in the *case* of their mother. Otherwise, the children of all of the wives in a household may have a *case* separate from the adult members of the compound.

By the age of six, young girls are taught by their mothers, grand-mother, or older sisters to perform small tasks around the household in order to prepare them for their future roles of mother and guardian of the household. They help clean the house, might accompany their mother to the market place, help do the cooking, etc.

Boys, when they are not attending school, are initiated in their father's trade. It is the male parent, relations, or older boys who assume the major responsibility in preparing the young boy for his role as a male member of the society.

This type of teaching/learning within the family or village is very informal and is based mostly—if not solely—on the modeling of activities and correction on the part of the elders and on observation and imitation by the young.

CCD/PC French — Unit IV
DAC-Dialogue Africain Contemporain — Page 10

## III. The School System

Before independence, the school system in the French-speaking West-African Nations was an exact replica of the French system. Since 1960, though the organization and the structure have remained unaltered, important changes in curriculum that take African realities and the specific needs of Africans more into account have been introduced—chiefly in such subjects as History, Geography, etc.

Compared to the American system, two obvious differences emerge: (1) Education is free at all levels. All types of scholarships are available for those who cannot afford the cost of books and other needed items. (2) The system is highly centralized: in a given country the same books and teaching materials are used everywhere, and the same exams are given throughout.

*Primary Education:* Primary education is now compulsory, at least in theory. Classes are generally large—30 to 40 or more pupils to a class. (Notice that in our lesson the *maître* has an unusually small class and he also serves as *directeur* of the school.) Children start at the age of six or seven. The primary school course lasts six years, at the end of which qualified students may take an exam to enter secondary or vocational schools.

*Secondary Education:* This type of education is provided at the *lycée, colleges,* and *cours complémentaires.*

*Lycée and Colleges:* All things considered, the difference between the two kinds of schools is administrative rather than academic. They both offer 7-year courses divided into two cycles. The first lasts four years, at the end of which students may take the B.E.P.C. ("Brevet d'études du premier cycle"). The second cycle takes three years and leads to the *Baccalaureat.* Success at this exam is generally the prerequisite for entrance at the University.

*Cours Complémentaires:* They offer a 4-year program similar to the first cycle of lycées and colleges.

*Vocational Schools:* These are basically *Technical Schools* and offer certificates and degrees in various technical fields.

*Higher Education:* French-speaking West Africa, so called, counts several Universities, the oldest of which is the University of Dakar. Most of these Universities have *facultés* of law, sciences, and letters offering courses leading to the *licence.* It is worth noting that a great number of French-speaking West African students are pursuing University studies abroad, mainly in France.

CCD/PC French
DAC-Dialogue Africain Contemporain

Unit IV
Page 12

## LECTURE.

### LE JOUEUR DE KORA.

Kwaku, un *joueur* (1) de Kora, voit Mamadou Diop et sa femme dans la cour.
Il entre dans la concession.
- "Bonjour, Mamadou! Comment *va* (2) la famille?"
- "Très bien, merci. Asseyez-vous ici, mon ami."
Kwaku prend place sur la natte à côté de Mamadou.
Il prend sa *Kora* (3) et *joue* (4).
Mamadou et sa femme *écoutent* (5).
Kwaku *raconte* (6) l'histoire du village.
Il raconte aussi l'histoire de la *vie* (7) du grand-père de Mamadou.
Les enfants de Mamadou n'*aiment* (8) pas beaucoup les histoires de Kwaku; ils ne *comprennent* (9) pas très bien.
*Mais* (10) ils aiment bien la musique de Kwaku.
Kwaku connaît beaucoup de vieilles *chansons* (11).
Kwaku *chante* (12).
Les enfants *arrêtent* (13) les *jeux* (14) et viennent tout près de lui.
Nabou, la femme de Mamadou, *apporte* (15) des *noix* (16) de cola.
La musique est très agréable.
Mamadou donne un boubou à Kwaku.
Kwaku *dit* (17) merci à la famille et *quitte* (18) la concession.

### VOCABULAIRE

1) Un joueur : player.
Ex: Kwaku est joueur de Kora.

2) Aller : (il/elle va): (to) go.
Here: "How *is* the family?"

3) Une Kora : Guitare africaine.
Ex: Les américains ne jouent pas de la Kora.

4) Jouer : (to) play.
Ex: Les enfants jouent dans la cour.

5) Ecouter : (to) listen.
Ex: Mamadou écoute la musique.



6) Raconter : (to) recount, tell.
Ex: Les maîtres racontent des histoires aux élèves.

7) Une vie : Life, lifetime.
Ex: La vie dans une concession est agréable.

8) Aimer : (to) like, love.
Ex: Kwaku aime les enfants de Mamadou.

9) Comprendre : (ils/elles comprennent): (to) understand.
Ex: Les élèves comprennent bien le français.

10) Mais : but. Conjunction indicating opposition.
Ex: Ma maison n'est pas grande, mais elle est agréable.

11) Une chanson : Song.
Ex: Je connais la chanson "La vie en rose".

12) Chanter : (to) sing.
Ex: Les élèves chantent en classe.

13) Arrêter : (to) stop.
Ex: Le chauffeur arrête son autobus.

14) Un jeu : (pluriel: jeux): game.
Ex: Je ne connais pas de jeux africains.

15) Apporter : (to) carry, bring.
Ex: Les enfants apportent des livres en classe.

16) Une noix : Nut, seed (of avocado, for example)
Ex: Mamadou mange des noix de cola.

17) Dire : (il/elle dit): say, tell.
Ex: Kwaku dit "Bonjour" à Mamadou et Nabou.

18) Quitter : Abandonner.
Ex: Les enfants quittent la maison et arrivent à l'école.

CCD/PC French — Unit IV
DAC-Dialogue Africain Contemporain — Page 14

QUESTIONS

1) *Quel est le nom du joueur de Kora?*
2) *Où est-ce que le joueur de Kora voit Mamadou et sa femme?*
3) *Qu'est-ce que Kwaku fait?*
4) *Qu'est-ce que Mamadou et sa femme font?*
5) *Qu'est-ce que Kwaku raconte?*
6) *Qu'est-ce que les enfants font?*
7) *Est-ce que les enfants de Mamadou aiment les histoires de Kwaku?*
8) *Les enfants comprennent les histoires?*
9) *Est-ce qu'ils aiment les chansons de Kwaku?*
10) *Kwaku connaît beaucoup de chansons?*

11) *Kwaku chante: Qu'est-ce que les enfants font?*

12) *Comment est la musique?*

13) *Qu'est-ce que Nabou apporte?*

14) *Qu'est-ce que Mamadou donne à Kwaku?*

15) *Qu'est-ce que Kwaku fait?*

CCD/PC French
DAC-Dialogue Africain Contemporain

Unit IV
Page 16

### EXERCISES

1) *In this reading exercise you have encountered 3 of the following forms, all of which belong to the same word family* (famille de mots):

| | | |
|---|---|---|
| (1) jouer (il joue) | - verb - | (to) play (he plays) |
| (2) un joueur | - noun - | a player |
| (3) un jouet | - noun - | a toy; i.e., something one plays with |
| (4) un jeu (des jeux) | - noun - | a game (games); i.e., something one plays. |

Let's look at just the first three forms for the time being. If we take a hypothetical form JOU- (which never occurs alone in a sentence) as the stem, we can add three different endings to get three different words.

| | | | | |
|---|---|---|---|---|
| stem + | -ER | verb infinitive suffix | →JOU- + -ER | → jouer |
| stem + | {-EUR (m.)<br>{-EUSE (f.) | noun agent or instrument suffix | →JOU- + -EUR<br>-EUSE | → joueur<br>→ joueuse |
| stem + | -ET | Noun diminutive suffix | →JOU- + -ET | → jouet |

Notice that the fourth form above (un jeu) follows a different kind of rule. No suffix is added to the hypothetical stem; instead the vowel sound within the stem itself is changed.

CCD/PC French — Unit IV
DAC-Dialogue Africain Contemporain — Page 17

JOU→jeu

Choose the appropriate words from the above family and fill in the blanks.

1. La fille ________ dans la cour.
2. Elle a un petit ________.
3. Kwaku est un ________ sénégalais.
4. C'est un ________ traditionnel.

2) *Now think back to the first reading selection for a minute. Remember Mor?* Mor est cultivateur. *Study the following word family.*

| | | |
|---|---|---|
| (1) cultiver | - verb - | (to) cultivate |
| (2) un cultivateur (une cultivatrice) | - noun - | a cultivator (farmer, grower) |
| (3) la culture | - noun - | cultivation |

What would you presume to be the stem in this family? (CULTIV-)

| | | | | |
|---|---|---|---|---|
| Stem + | -ER | verb infinitive suffix | →CULTIV- +-ER | →cultiver |
| Stem + | {-ATEUR (m.)<br>{-ATRICE (f.) | noun profession or object suffix | →CULTIV- + --ATEUR<br>-ATRICE | →cultivateur<br>→cultivatrice |

For the third form (la culture), notice that again no suffix is added to the hypothetical stem; instead, there is an internal change in the stem itself:

CULTIV→Culture

*Fill in the blanks:*

1. La ________ des plantes me plaît beaucoup.
2. Abou est un ________ traditionnel.
3. Il ________ des plantes près de sa concession.

3) *There are two forms of another word family used in*

*this reading selection. The hypothetical stem of these two forms might begin* CHAN-. *Fill in the blanks.*

Verb: ________

Noun: Une________

Kwaku joue de la Kora et ________.

Les enfants aiment les ________ de Kwaku.

4) *Find a verb in the reading that belongs to the same word family as the underlined noun in sentence (a). Fill in the blank in sentence (b) with the appropriate form of that verb.*

a) Il y a un arrêt d'autobus près d'ici?
b) Kwaku ________ l'autobus devant la concession de Mamadou.

---

The reader should again note that *Dialogue Africain Contemporain* teaches standard French but in a different cultural milieu. This permits parallel *language* courses with a different cultural emphasis or provides for the moving back and forth between cultures as a course progresses. This linear language progression would permit exposure of the student to facets of both European and African French cultures without inhibiting progression in the language skills.

# A Generative Approach—One More Time

A "Generative" approach is predicated upon three basic assumptions:

(1) *The person who really knows a language can*—either intuitively or through a series of implicit or explicit interrogations—*analyze utterances to the "Deep Structure" level.* The main immediate constituents are immediately apparent; if not, he can determine them. A language learner will maximize success when he develops this facility.

(2) *The language learner should be consciously involved in the learning quest.* He should know specifically (a) what he is looking for in a new segment of language; (b) how to isolate it; and (c) how to relate new language to that which he already can use.

(3) *Language generates only language.* The proper response to an utterance is another utterance, not repetition—language is communicative. The learning sequence should be aimed for learner performance of a particular language segment as a response to a communicative utterance.

These assumptions can be made reality entirely within a structured learning situation that is considerably more free and more efficient than other approaches yet developed. The end result is that the learner is able to react to a situation the same way as the native speaker within, of course, the domain of his experience and exposure to the target language—a restraint within which even the "native" must operate, by the way.

Finally, the only proper response to a unit of language, even if it is incomprehensible, is a purposeful reply.

## Does it Work?

"Does it work?" is the real consideration for the teacher. Accountability is a valid concept, and learner performance the ultimate criterion. "Does it work?"—"Yes, and well."

Pre-publication trials of materials based on a "Generative" approach in such diverse languages as Korean and Portuguese have demonstrated results. Increased effective language ability is complemented by enhanced learner interest and motivation.

In a sixty-hour Korean experiment, a student from an audio-lingual "control" class was overheard to remark to a "Generative" friend at the end of the first day of instruction, "Don't tell me you are *talking* to each other already?" Yes, they were—and they continued to speak Korean meaningfully for several weeks while the "control" classes progressed through the "ritual chanting" associated with classroom memorization in the audio-lingual approach.

"Generative" Korean students were enthusiastic and highly motivated. The evaluation showed that better students might have progressed faster than they did. Students who were used to active communication felt "turned off" when they had to rejoin their "audio-lingual" colleagues in a memorization-emphasis approach.

A full Peace Corps training program in Brazilian Portuguese used instructional materials based upon the "Generative" approach. Learners, mostly engineers and their wives, achieved an average Foreign Service speaking rating of 2-High after only two hundred and twenty hours of instruction; three hundred hours is usually required to reach this level. The materials received praise from both involved instructors and outside evaluators. The "Generative" PORTUGUÊS DO BRASIL: LINGUA E CULTURA* by Maria Chapira immediately retired the old Peace Corps standby, an "audio-lingual" text in use for several years.

Problems *were* encountered—the kind of problem dreamed of by educators—caused by the freedom and creativity offered to the teacher accustomed to the rigidity established by the behavioristic patterning framework of the audio-lingual approach. The problem was not "How do I gain flexibility?" but "What do I do with it now that I've got it?" The challenge to the individual teacher's creativity was not small—some teachers found themselves pressed to devise ways for providing for all the communication their students were capable of. Students *could* talk—teachers had to find things for them *to talk about.*

A "Generative" approach has a geometric expansion, limited only by the creativity and flexibility of the individuals involved within the framework of their linguistic competence. It does work, and well, but teachers who are reluctant to really involve themselves in speaking their foreign language should perhaps think twice before attempting it. The "Generative" approach *forces* communication—and the foreign-language teacher must now become involved, not as a "model" but as a "person."

In the "Generative" approach, the teacher becomes an active guide, a patient but persistent interactor. Gone is the day of one-way mimicry, repetition, and imitation—language learning now becomes the communicative process that is language by definition. *Language learning* simply becomes *language beginning.*

*The Center for Curriculum Development, Inc., Philadelphia, Pa.

# References

Ausubel, David P. "Adults versus Children in Second Language Learning: Psychological Considerations," *Modern Language Journal,* XLVIII, 7 (Nov. 1964), pp. 420-424.

Bazan, Beverly M. "The Danger of Assumption without Proof," *Modern Language Journal,* XLVIII, 6 (Oct. 1964).

Bever, T. G. "Cognitive Basis of Linguistic Processing," in Hayes, J. (ed.) *Cognition and Language Learning* (New York: Wiley, 1970).

Bloom, Benjamin. "Learning for Mastery," *Evaluation Comment,* Vol. I, 2 (May, 1968), (Los Angeles: UCLA Center for the Evaluation of Instructional Programs), p. 1.

Brooks, Nelson. *Language and Language Learning* (New York: Harcourt, Brace and World, 1961).

______. "Language Teaching: The New Approach," *Phi Delta Kappan,* March, 1966, pp. 357-359.

Carroll, John B. "Contributions of Psychological Theory and Educational Research to the Teaching of Foreign Languages," *Modern Language Journal,* XLIX/5 (May, 1965).

______. "Research in the Teaching of Foreign Languages," in N. Gage (ed.) *Handbook of Research on Teaching* Chicago: Rand McNally, 1963).

Chomsky, Noam. "A Review of B. F. Skinner's Verbal Behavior," in Fodor and Katz, *The Structure of Language* (Englewood Cliffs, N. J.: Prentice-Hall, 1964).

Conbach, L. J. *Educational Psychology,* 2nd ed. (New York: Harcourt, Brace and World, 1963).

Cook, Walter. *Introduction to Tagmemic Analysis* (New York: Holt, Rinehart and Winston, 1969).

del Olmo, Guillermo. "Professional and Pragmatic Perspectives on the Audiolingual Approach: Introduction and Review," *Foreign Language Annals,* Vol. II, no.1 (Oct. 1968).

Fillmore, Charles. "The Case for Case," in Bach, E. and Harms, R. (eds.), *Universals in Linguistic Theory* (New York: Holt, Rinehart & Winston, 1968).

Finocchario, M. "Myths of Language Teaching." Address to TESOL section, 1971 ACTFL meeting, Los Angeles, November 1971.

Fraser, Bruce. "Linguistics and the EFL Teacher," in Lugton, R. (ed.), *Preparing the EFL Teacher: A Projection for the '70's*

(Philadelphia: Center for Curriculum Development, 1970), pp. 1-27.

Frymier, Jack R. *Motivation: The Mainspring of Learning.* Monograph written for the Bureau of Research, Department of Public Instruction, Harrisburg, Pa., 1968.

Gamlin, P. "First and Second Language Acquisition," in H. Stern (ed.), *Perspectives on Second Language Teaching* (Toronto: OISE, 1970).

Guba, Egon G. "Methodological Strategies for Educational Changes." A paper presented to the Conference on Strategies for Educational Change, Washington, D. C., Nov. 8-10, 1965. Mimeo.

Hale, Thomas and Budar, Eva. "Are TESOL Classes the Only Answer?" *Modern Language Journal,* Vol. LIV, no. 7 (Nov. 1970), pp. 487-492.

Jakobovits, Leon. *Foreign Language Learning* (Rowley, Mass.: Newbury House Publishers, 1970).

______. "The Physiology and Psychology of Second Language Learning," in Birkmeier, E. (ed.), *Britannica Review of Foreign Language Education,* Vol. I (Chicago: Encyclopedia Britannica, 1969).

Lado, Robert. *Language Teaching: A Scientific Approach* (New York: McGraw-Hill, 1964).

Lakoff, George. *Deep Surface Grammar* (Bloomington, Ind.: The Linguistics Club, Indiana University, 1968). 75pp. mimeo.

Lenneberg, Eric "The Capacity for Language Acquisition," in Fodor and Katz (eds.), *The Structure of Language* (Englewood Cliffs, N.J.: Prentice-Hall, 1964), pp. 579-603.

McDonald,F. J. *Educational Psychology,* 2nd ed. (Belmont Calif.: Wadworth Publishing Co., 1965).

Maslow, A. H. " A Theory of Human Motivation," *Psychology Review,* 50 (1943), pp. 370-396.

Mathiot, Madeleine. *An Approach to the Cognitive Study of Language* (Bloomington, Ind.: Indiana University, 1968).

O'Neil, Wayne. "The Export of TESOL: Are Audio-Lingual Techniques Universally Appropriate?" *Language Research Report No. 2* (Cambridge, Mass.: Language Research Foundation, 1970), pp. 1-8.

Olsson, Margareta. *Implicit and Explicit: Göteborg, Undervisnings Metod: Engelska* No. 3. (Götteborg, Sweden: Göthenburg University Dept. of Educational Research, 1969).

Parent, P. Paul and Belasco, Simon. "Parallel-Column Bilingual

Reading Materials as a Pedagogical Device: An Experimental Evaluation," *Modern Language Journal,* Vol. LIV, No. 7 (Nov. 1970), pp. 493-504.

Pimsleur, Paul; Mosberg, L. and Morrison, A. "Student Factors in Foreign Language Learning: A Review of the Literature," *Modern Language Journal,* April, 1962, pp. 160-170.

Renard, C. and Heinle, C. H. *Implementing VOIX ET IMAGES DE FRANCE in American Schools and Colleges* (Philadelphia: Center for Curriculum Development, 1969).

Rivers, Wilga. *The Psychologist and the Foreign Language Teacher* (Chicago: University of Chicago Press, 1964).

Scott, Charles. "Transformational Theory and English as a Second Language/Dialect," in Atlatis, James (ed.) *Report of the Twentieth Annual Round Table Meeting on Linguistics and Language Studies* (Washington, D. C.: Georgetown University Press, 1970).

Seuren, Pieter A. M. *Operators and Nucleus* (Cambridge: University Press, 1969).

Smith, Philip D. *An Assessment of Three Foreign Language Teaching Strategies Utilizing Three Language Laboratory Systems.* Final Report of USOE Project S-0683. 1968.

———. *A Comparison of the Cognitive and Audiolingual Approaches to Foreign Language Instruction* (Philadelphia: Center for Curriculum Development, 1970).

Sparkman, Colley F. "Teaching Students to Read a Foreign Language *versus* Letting Them Learn How?" *Modern Language Journal,* Vol. XV, no. 3 (Dec. 1930), p. 170.

———. "A New Language Must be Spliced Onto One's Native Language," *Modern Language Journal,* Vol. XXXIII, No. 5 (May, 1949), pp. 355-362.

Spolsky, Bernard. "Linguistics and Language Pedagogy—applications of Implications," in Atlatis, James (ed.), *Report of the Twentieth Round Table Meeting on Linguistics and Language Studies* (Washington, D.C.: Georgetown University Press, 1970).

Stein, H. H. *Perspectives on Second Language Teaching* (Toronto: Ontario Institute for Studies in Education, 1970).

Steinkrauss, W. "Psycholinguistics and Second Language Teaching," in H. Stern (ed.) *Perspectives on Second Language Teaching* (Toronto: OISE, 1970).

Valdman, Albert. *Recent Trends in Language Learning* (New York: McGraw-Hill, 1966).